GOING PRO
IN LIFE

LEVERAGING YOUR
STUDENT-ATHLETE EXPERIENCE
FOR SUCCESS AFTER COLLEGE

ANDY DINKIN

FOREWORD BY COACH MACK BROWN

NORTHWESTERN MUTUAL – CHARLOTTE
RICHARD WORRELL, CFP / MANAGING PARTNER
richard.worrell@nm.com / Office 704-365-2014

SPARK Publications
Charlotte, North Carolina

Going Pro in Life: Leveraging Your Student-Athlete Experience for Success After College
Andy Dinkin

Designed, produced, and published by
SPARK Publications, SPARKpublications.com
Charlotte, North Carolina

Printed in the United States of America.
Paperback, February 2020, ISBN: 978-1-943070-62-6
Library of Congress Control Number: 2019905728

Acknowledgments & Dedication

L ooking back on my life, I feel blessed to have been coached and mentored by so many great people, and their wisdom is found throughout this book. This includes Paul Foringer, Jonathan Cole, Wilbur Givens, Armin Moshyedi, Mark Dove, Rip Matthews, Rich Tuten, Brian Davis, John Blanchard, Steve Steinbacher, Pat Crowley, Carlton Bailey, Richard Applebaum, Jeff Garnica, Allan Gorry, Tim Goad, David Finch, John Black, Lou Solomon, David Kossove, Jeffrey Gitomer, Howard Winokuer, Rick Kramer, Leighton Cubbage, Rabbi Nate Segal, Daniel Levine, Frank Wilson, Bob Salvin, and Alex Simakas, my gracious recruiting host and the main reason I chose to attend the University of North Carolina at Chapel Hill.

Special thanks to my dear friend Hans Rehme, who saw more in me than I saw in myself and whose friendship strengthened me to develop as a high school football player and person. He and my wonderful high school coach, Fred Shepherd, made it possible for me to play in college.

I also want to thank Greg Dinkin, Michael Benefield, Rabbi Chanoch Oppenheim, Bill Whitley, Melisa Graham, and the entire team at SPARK Publications, all of whom made significant contributions to this book. And of course, a big thanks to Coach Mack Brown for writing the foreword and, more importantly, teaching me the importance of having a positive attitude for positive results.

Countless friends and teammates have helped me get to where I am today. If you are mad about not being named, you are among the countless.

Last but not least, I want to dedicate this book to my family: my grandparents of blessed memory, the Osterneck family of blessed memory, my supportive parents and in-laws, my great kids, Jayme and Drew, and my loving wife, Leslie.

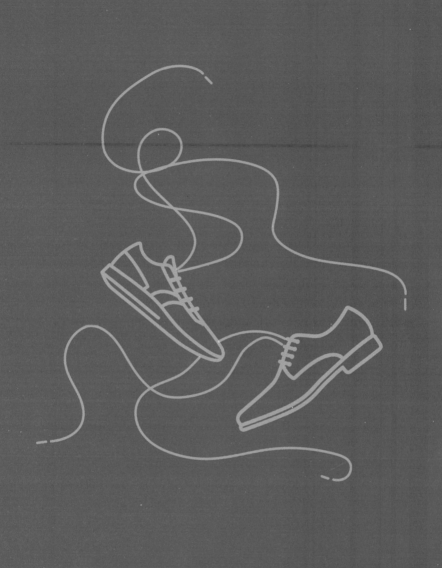

Table of Contents

Rules of the Game

Write in this book.
You'll see "Build Your Game Plan" exercises throughout the book to help you process the information presented and plan your next steps. Take advantage of those moments of reflection and feel free to write directly in the book. If you don't own this book or would like an alternative to writing in it, see below.

Download the "Build Your Game Plan" exercises as a separate booklet.
All of the exercises are also collected in a downloadable PDF playbook available at goingproinlife.com/gameplan for the low price of your email address.

Review the "Replay" summaries.

At the end of each chapter you will find a "Replay" summary of the chapter's key points. If you need a refresher after you've completed the book, read the replays. But this book is just the beginning. If you want to really excel, invest in the video training and coaching opportunities available at goingproinlife.com.

Translate your athletic skills.

No matter your circumstances or background, you have the talent to go pro in life. It just takes some self-awareness, planning, and willingness to do the work—skills you practice every day in your chosen sport. This book and the additional training materials help you translate those skills and your dedication into the working world.

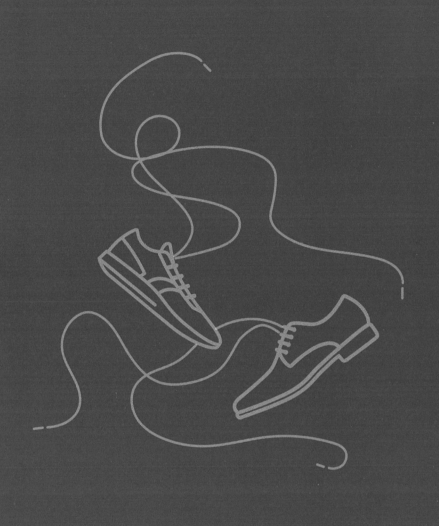

Foreword

I have been coaching college football for over forty years. People think that to be qualified for this job, you need to be able to come up with great plays, design the right workouts, think on your feet, and deal with stress and other aspects of coaching. Although these are crucial qualities for a college football coach, one thing most people don't consider is that the coach has to have the ability—almost a sixth sense—to know whom to recruit. I never looked for just how well the guy could play; it was equally important for me to be confident that he would be a team player and fit into the culture that the coaching staff worked hard to create. I am responsible for the public and sometimes private behavior of the players as long as they are on the team. But there's another aspect of our student-athletes' lives that neither I nor most others considered when entering the vocation of coaching, and it is one of the most crucial parts of the athlete's life.

It's a question that few want to ask, but it must be asked: what will our players do at the end of four or five years on our team? Very few will play in the pros, and even if one is fortunate enough to be part of that privileged group, he most likely will not be in the pros for more than a few years and will not have accumulated enough income to support himself for too long when he leaves. The athletes we read about who are making millions each year are a tiny minority. What happens to the guys who didn't make it to the pros or had a short professional football career? To my knowledge, no one has ever addressed this question in a formal manner or offered guidance to these players, who are the overwhelming majority of all college athletes.

Finally, someone has been willing to take the time and thought to this crucial challenge, and I am proud to say that I was once his coach. Andy Dinkin played Tar Heel football for five seasons; he has much in common with today's players and is willing to tackle this issue. He was in their shoes, had the same hopes and dreams, but ultimately realized that he would have to support himself and find fulfillment in life with something other than football. He is one of the only players I have ever met who took a commission-only job straight out of college. He had other offers, but he chose a path that would require the same grit and determination needed for an offensive lineman, a position he fought hard for season after season. He had developed an incredible work ethic when he played at Carolina; his mind and body were products of years of pushing himself to be the best he could. Now, he has decided to share the fruit of his twenty years of entrepreneurial, consulting, and strategic experience. In addition to the world of business, he has been actively involved with the nonprofit sector, and among other things, he was the board chairman of Girls on the Run, a national organization whose mission is to teach life skills to girls and give them the confidence to make their marks in the world. He has also chaired and consulted organizations in his faith-based community.

When Andy told me about his idea, I invited him to give a presentation at UNC. The response from the players and coaches was overwhelming. I knew this was an important subject, but I didn't expect this reaction. After his talk, one of my coaches commented that he had never seen so many players participate and be engaged at a presentation.

Several players emailed Andy afterward and are already implementing his methods and heeding his advice, and as word gets out, more players seek his guidance.

Who is this book for? Not just student-athletes. Mothers, fathers, aunts, uncles, friends, and anyone else who wants to help a young adult find his or her way into a world foreign to them. Most athletes' lives have been regulated since high school, and when they get to college, it's regulated more. What they eat, when they eat, when they sleep, and where and when they have to be at practice and class are things they never had to think about. After college, they are now thrust into a world without regulation, and it's up to them to figure it out and make something of it. I recommend this book as the first step in navigating this unknown journey in which they now find themselves. Andy's message is so clear that I would recommend it to any college student, even a non-athlete, who wants to make sure he or she has a job waiting after graduation—but not just any job, their dream job. This isn't just material to make you feel good; it's real guidance for students willing to be coached. The earlier you begin—his plan starts with freshman year—the more you benefit.

Andy Dinkin has done a great service to young athletes everywhere. Although they don't think of it now, in a few years, most of them will no longer be playing in stadiums and arenas for thousands of people; they will be earning a living some other way. It is my fervent hope that you read and implement the ideas in this book and share them with others.

The iconic Vince Lombardi once commented, "The price of success is hard work, dedication to the job at hand, and the determination that whether we win or lose, we have applied the best of ourselves to the task at hand." If you want the best for yourself or someone you care for, grab this book and don't put it down until you can apply its contents. Being a winner on the court, rink, mat, or field was important during college, but now it's time to be a winner in the game of life.

Respectfully,
Mack Brown
Head Football Coach
University of North Carolina at Chapel Hill
College Football Hall of Fame, Class of 2018

Introduction

You're a big deal on campus right now. What you may not be aware of is that the moment you leave campus, your glory will fade. I say this not as a warning but as an *opportunity*. You have no idea of the opportunities available to you as a student-athlete. People love sports and hold you in high regard. There are fans and alumni who take a special interest in your life ... right now. Once you graduate, many of those opportunities will be lost. That is, unless you have a game plan like the one offered in this book.

I dreamed of playing in the NFL. And though, like you, I did everything in my power to excel in sports, I couldn't make a living playing the game. Thankfully, I did things off the field that put me in the enviable position of:

- Having several valuable internships during college.
- Finding mentors who made key introductions and offered guidance and wisdom.
- Creating a bidding war amongst several employers upon graduation.
- Discovering my post-athletic calling and doing work I've loved for the past twenty-five years.
- Having meaningful relationships with my college teammates, coaches, and friends that provide ongoing personal fulfillment and professional value.

The best part about what I did is that it's simple to execute—not *easy* but simple. Everything you need to know is in the following pages. And since you're an athlete, I know you possess the grit and discipline to execute the game plan.

Any fool can find a job. Your goal is to explore your career options firsthand, before you graduate, and learn what excites you and what you have a talent and a joy for doing. I will show you step-by-step how to use your status as a college student-athlete to meet the right people and build the meaningful relationships you need to discover your professional passions and land a promising job that positions you for growth and success.

Learn from My Story

It was 1992, and finally, after five years, including many sessions of summer school, I had earned my degree from the University of North Carolina at Chapel Hill. I remember staring at my diploma for the first time and thinking, "Wow, a Bachelor of Arts. What in the world are they talking about?" There was nothing about my time in college that seemed particularly artful, but the bachelor part certainly had a familiar ring to it.

You see, when I was in college, my first priority was playing football. Class work was secondary. I *loved* football, and I had convinced myself that when I graduated, I would keep playing football as a professional. Because of this expectation, I spent more time engaged in athletics than in academics.

Unfortunately for me, when my senior season ended, no NFL scouts came looking for me. I soon learned that only 200 of the approximately 9,000 kids that play college football each season make the NFL. So there I was, 280 pounds, and my best skills were reading a linebacker blitz and devouring an all-you-can-eat buffet. How in the world was I ever going to find a job?

Fortunately, I had some prior exposure to the professional world and had made some meaningful relationships. So when my NFL career never materialized, I already had an idea of what I wanted to do, and I had people who were willing to help me in this pursuit.

Many of you are probably asking yourself a similar question: how will I find a job when I get out of college? And while this is a very important question to ask, it's the wrong question. The right question to ask: what would I love to do as a career?

The problem is, nobody knows. A bigger problem is that people often confuse what they love to do for recreation as something they can make a career of. You have people who love the outdoors becoming park rangers, only to find out that they've signed on for a desk job that requires a tremendous amount of paperwork. Or you'll find someone who loves sports becoming a sports agent, only to realize that most of their work involves reading legal contracts.

In my case, long before I graduated, I stopped asking how I was going to find a job, and I started asking how I was going to find something I loved as much as playing football. Playing college football required a ton of work—6 a.m. weight lifting, three-hour practices, grueling off-season conditioning programs, and long hours watching game film, all while still carrying a full course load. And you know what? I loved every minute of it!

The entire experience taught me that if you love what you do, you'll never work a day in your life. I knew I'd be miserable if I didn't find something that I had a passion for.

So how did I go about discovering what I'd love to do for a career, and how did I land my first job? In *Going Pro in Life*, you'll learn exactly how I did it. If you are one of the 99 percent of male or female college athletes who love your sport and are committed to it but most likely will not make a career out of it, you will need a guide to help you harness your talent and learn how to leverage it for your benefit. This book will teach you how to proactively use your athletic background to your benefit. Because your time is in high demand, this book is designed to be read in a few hours. Simply reading it, however, is not going to cut it. This is a *workbook*. Its success is dependent on you doing the exercises and following through on the promises you make to yourself.

It is the first step in creating a game plan that will put you on the fast track to a great career after graduation. Read it all the way through once, then refer back to the chapters as you come to these points in the real world. If you want to have real success, it will serve you well to keep coming back to this book. In addition to this book, resources are also available to you at goingproinlife.com.

The ideas presented in this book are the result of over twenty-five years of my own personal research and experiences. I've been where you are right now, and I've been in the workforce hiring people like you since I graduated. I know that this advice will make a positive difference for all college student-athletes who take the time to read it and an even greater difference for those who implement the strategies presented.

My personal journey has taught me how others can get the most out of their college athletic experience, and I thank you for giving me the opportunity to share this wisdom. It is my dream that all student-athletes live up to their full potential. I hope this book will be a valuable guide throughout your college career and that you will use it to seize opportunities and avoid pitfalls. This book is your career launch formula for obtaining a fulfilling career.

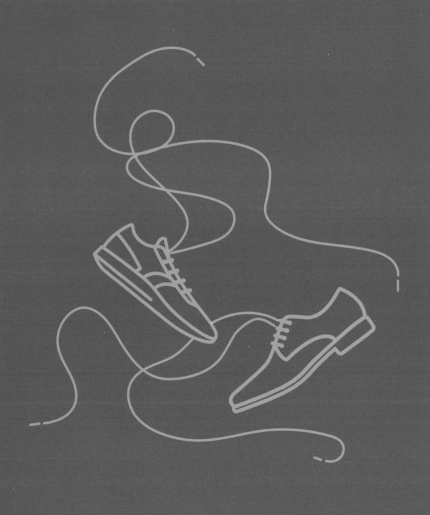

CHAPTER

1

Understand the Purpose of College

Collage is great time to learn about yourself, gain independence, develop life-long friendships, and have fun. The true purpose of college, however, is discovering what you love to do and are good at. It is also to gain the knowledge and resources to enter into a fulfilling career upon graduation.

Many students lose sight of this purpose, and when they graduate, they have no idea what they want to do or how they will find a job doing it. This is a big problem. If you don't know what you love to do, how will you find out? Once you determine your "job goal," how will you land the job?

College student-athletes have opportunities and resources that are unavailable to their fellow classmates to help get answers to these important questions. Our culture has tremendous passion for athletics and great interest in its participants. Right now, there are supporters of your sports program willing to go above and beyond to help you.

But you won't be a college student-athlete forever, and if you don't have a game plan for how to best capitalize on your current level of status, the window of opportunity will close quickly. Unfortunately, the fans, alumni, professors, students, and boosters who can't get enough of you now won't have the same level of interest in you once your athletic career is over.

If you're smart—and I know you are, or you would not be reading this book—you need to understand and act on these four basic truths about your current status as a college student-athlete:

1. It won't last forever (really).
2. People care more about you right now than they will when you finish your playing career.
3. Don't expect doors to open up for you just because you play a college sport. You can leverage your experience to open doors, but they won't just swing open for you. To set yourself up for a great future, you need to establish as many meaningful relationships as you can with those who are interested in you now. These are the folks who are in a position to help you after your playing career is over.
4. The sooner you discover your career passion, the sooner you can hone your purpose.

Rev Your Engine

When a plane is ready to take off, it has to build up speed quickly. The pilot must really pour it on in order to gain altitude. Takeoff is tough; it's intense. Windows are rattling, luggage is shifting, ears are popping—you know something is going on. If the pilot doesn't build up enough speed at takeoff, they'll have to work even harder to gain altitude.

It's the same with starting your career. Most people don't put in the necessary work at the beginning. They just "fall" into their first jobs and face a long, slow climb out. They never pour it on to achieve the high altitude they seek. The few who understand the importance of finding out what they love before they accept a job are the ones who gain altitude quickly and ultimately soar.

Takeoff is a lot of work, but it's for a relatively short period of time. This is where you set your trajectory. Don't you want to soar instead of scraping by doing something you don't like? Put in the effort now—while you're still in college—and watch what happens.

Getting off to a good start is important in anything you do in life. As a college student-athlete, a good start can make a difference in how well you do academically, athletically, and personally over the course of the next four or five years.

I saw many teammates get into so much trouble academically their first year that the grade point average they strived for became unobtainable. I also saw freshmen who made such a poor impression on the coaches, upperclassmen, managers, trainers, and other students that they were never truly accepted or respected. Now, this isn't to say that one can't make up for a poor start, but college can be a lot easier if you come out of the gate quickly.

The most important rule for a freshman member of a team: it is better to be seen, not heard. It's a solid rule for a new employee as well. In the presence of upperclassmen and coaches, choose your words carefully. As I learned early on, there is nothing worse than a loud-mouthed freshman. It's too bad some of my teammates didn't learn this until it was too late and after their reputations were ruined.

I remember the time when my freshmen teammates and I had to stand in front of the entire team and individually introduce ourselves to all the upperclassmen. Some guys were very modest and soft-spoken during their introductions, while others were loud and cocky. I assure you that my loud, cocky teammates were not well received. In thirty seconds' time, a lot of my friends had established a poor reputation that was tough to erase.

What's the secret to gaining the respect of your teammates and others? Earn it. Don't tell people how great you are; show them. What many freshmen athletes fail to realize is that most of their teammates at the college level were once high school standouts like them. Bragging about your state championship victory or telling stories about all the schools that recruited you is a surefire way to make a bad impression.

The best approach for gaining the respect of the upperclassmen is simply to do as you are told, arrive early and stay late, show a positive attitude, work hard at practice, show up at class, and don't pester them with too many questions until you've earned their respect. If you follow the key rule of "being seen and not heard," you will carve your niche and be able to show your true colors. In time, you will be able to ask all the questions you want. Curiosity is an asset for newbies both on a sports team and in the office—just remember to *lead with value and work ethic.*

If you want to make an impression on one of the respected members of the team—whether it's the team captain or a partner at a law firm—offer to make their job easier. Volunteer to pitch batting practice for one of the seniors. It's the equivalent of offering to write up and distribute meeting notes for one of the law firm's partners.

In terms of academics, be sure not to dig a hole for yourself early on in your college career. Being a freshman means a lot of new distractions. Depending on your background, you may be experiencing a number of things for the very first time. Your freshman year is an exciting time, and by all means enjoy yourself. However, you must still keep on top of your studies and your responsibilities to your team.

This four- or five-year period of your life is when you must work the hardest. You must really "rev your engine" now, while so many valuable resources and meaningful relationships are readily accessible to you. Do what I tell you in this book and set yourself up to soar to great professional heights for the rest of your career.

Find a Mentor

As you probably have already learned at this point in your life, experience is the best teacher. If you don't currently have experience in the area in which you are trying to excel, why not find a person who does have experience to help you?

Throughout my life, I have been able to grow a great deal as a person because of some very strong mentor relationships. Never did I learn more valuable lessons than those taught to me by a trusted upperclassman early on in my college career. A good mentor can help you answer a wide variety of questions—everything from where to get a good burger on campus to how to handle an issue with a particular coach, where to look for summer employment, and which professors are the most interesting.

Since the advice of a mentor is so valuable, it's important to find the right one. If a relationship with open lines of communication doesn't naturally evolve between you and an upperclassman, then begin to seek a mentor on your own. Attributes such as honesty, work ethic, and kindness should be at the forefront in your selection process. I recommend taking a good look at the respect a potential student-athlete mentor has from the coaches and other teammates. This is an excellent indication of whether the person you are considering has good character or not.

One place to start looking is with the person who served as your recruiting host. Coaches like to match recruits with a host of similar qualities. Should that be the situation, and assuming you got along well with your recruiting host, then you are off to a strong start.

I was lucky. My recruiting host, Alex, turned out to be not only a great mentor but also a trusted friend. Alex was able to teach me a tremendous amount about dedication, work ethic, and kindness. By following his example and listening to his advice, I was able to clearly navigate through some very difficult situations during my college career, particularly when I changed positions, which was a challenging transition. Whether it was an unexpected position change, an injury, or just plain old homesickness, Alex was always there to provide meaningful support. Through our sharing, we were able to develop the type of friendship that will last forever. Never was I more honored than when my mentor asked me to be in his wedding. Today, Alex is one of my most trusted business advisors, someone who has helped me review contracts and referred me to the very best legal counsel.

If your recruiting host is not the right match, handpick your own mentor based on the criteria I set earlier. Consider asking your coach or academic advisor for a suggestion. Perhaps the teammate directly ahead of you on the depth chart is the perfect mentor, but recognize that this person may feel threatened by you, which could tarnish their advice, so choose wisely.

Once you have a person in mind, test the potential relationship by asking for advice on some minor issues. Ask for a course recommendation or a good place to eat. If you have chosen the right person, he or she will be happy to answer.

Lead with value! Don't simply ask someone to be your mentor. Go to them with a solution to one of their problems or a way to help. From there, the relationship will either flourish or fail. Above all else, be yourself. There is no sense in building a relationship with someone based on a false persona. More than likely, the upperclassman you are confiding in had the same questions and insecurities as a freshman. Speak freely and openly about what is on your mind. If you don't click with your first potential mentor, continue looking.

As my college career developed, I had a number of mentors. Some I went to for advice about football, and others gave me valuable insight into helping solve problems in different areas of my life. The key is to find people you can trust and whose opinion you respect. A good mentor can help you learn "the ropes" in half the time it normally takes.

I also suggest finding a mentor among the academic faculty on campus. This is important for socialization into a profession other than sports. If you have an idea of what field you would like to be in after graduation, make friends with a teacher in that department or a professional working in that field. He or she can offer valuable insight about courses, internships, and career opportunities. Don't stop looking until you find people who will make a positive difference in your life.

Once you find those people, treat them like gold and work hard to help them accomplish their goals. The first question on everyone's mind when you first meet: what's in it for me? That's why I can't stress enough the importance of leading with value. Again, you are in a unique position, so leverage the tools at your disposal. You can invite a professor or other mentor to practice. Or you may be able to get a sideline pass for his or her kids. Non-athletes don't have this advantage. The small gesture you make now may be your meal ticket two years from now. *Seize these opportunities!*

As you progress in your college career, be receptive to those seeking your advice and look to build friendships with those whom you can mentor. The underclassman you help will go on to do great things, and those relationships will benefit you for a lifetime.

Overcome a Poor Start

If you got off to a poor start, take heart. No game is decided by one bad play. If you made a bad first impression, publicly acknowledge your shortcoming and ask for forgiveness. Then consistently demonstrate your positive personality traits—the impression you prefer people to have of you. While the bad impression only took a few seconds, creating a new, positive impression will require time and persistence. If you're having trouble with a particular person, make an effort to grow closer to that person or to make their life easier. What value can you offer them, or how can you help them feel valued?

If you find yourself in an academic hole, start by determining the cause of your low GPA and meeting with your academic advisor to form a plan. Are you struggling in one particular subject or all of your classes? If it's a particular class, tutoring can go a long way. Your advisor can connect you with peer tutoring. Trouble in all of your classes probably means you haven't put in the time to study. Sign up for mandatory study hall and talk to your professors about extra work that could increase your GPA. When you talk to your professors, make sure it's during their office hours when their attention can be focused on you. Be humble and accept responsibility for the position you're in. And then follow through on any opportunities or extra work you're given to improve your grades.

⟳▶ Replay

Start now. Don't wait until the semester before graduation to start building relationships. Effective networking means creating contacts and relationships while you are still in school. The earlier in your career, the better. That way you have more time to solidify the relationship. If you are a senior, you must double or triple your efforts immediately. If you are a freshman, don't procrastinate. Take the lessons from this book and implement them quickly.

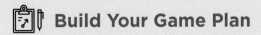 **Build Your Game Plan**

Based on the criteria you have set for choosing a mentor, list some potential candidates to fill that position in your life.

1.
2.
3.
4.
5.
6.
7.
8.
9.
10.

List questions or challenges that a good mentor could help you with.

1.
2.
3.
4.
5.
6.
7.
8.
9.
10.

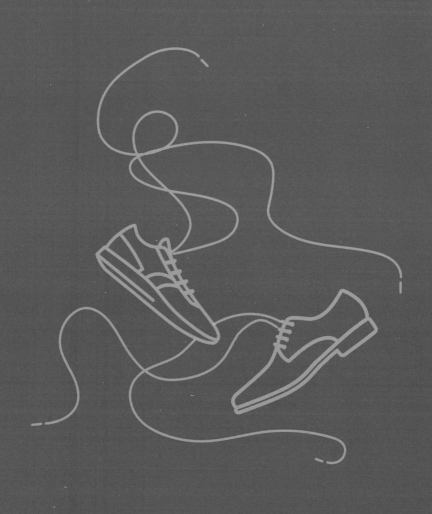

2

Set Your College Goals

A goal is a clear vision of where you want to be in a finite period of time. It is a constant, sometimes consuming presence that allows you to make the necessary choices and sacrifices in order to achieve that vision. A true goal will influence even the most minor decisions in your life and at times will dominate your entire existence.

If this definition sounds a bit dramatic, you may be confusing "desires" for "goals." Desires are what you dream for; goals are what you plan for and work toward achieving. You must "plan and do" not "hope and pray." There is a big difference.

This explains why many people struggle to lose weight. At some point in our lives, many of us have said, "My goal is to lose five pounds." Yet within a day, or sometimes within the hour, we will eat food that we know is unhealthy. Losing weight was not a goal but a desire. Achieving a goal requires willingness to make sacrifices. In the weight-loss example, we were not willing to forgo the instant gratification of a cupcake (or milkshake or whatever your poison) in order to reach a long-term objective.

SMART Goal

Specific description of who, what, where, and why
Measurable progression from point A to point B
Achievable but still challenging
Relevant to your ultimate long-term plan
Timely with a specific end date

Example goal:

I will achieve a 3.0 grade point average or better by the end of the academic year, so I can make the Atlantic Coast Conference Academic Honor Roll. I will reach my goal by attending classes, taking great notes, attending all study sessions, completing all assignments to the best of my ability, and asking for tutoring if my assignment grades aren't in line with my goal or if I find the material difficult.

If you learn the skills required to plan, implement, and achieve your goals, you will have a skill set that will serve you well during college and throughout your entire life. How will you measure your success if you have no clear idea of where you want to be? For this reason alone, it is important to set some clear goals for your college career and beyond.

There are many schools of thought about how to set a goal. Some will tell you that it is imperative to write your goals out and carry them with you at all times. Others say that you must evaluate your accomplishments on a daily basis and set new goals accordingly. Another method prescribes that you set a series of short-term goals in order to reach your long-term objectives. If you are currently using any of these principles effectively, then by all means continue to do what works. If you have not set any goals for yourself, then let me make a few suggestions.

Segment Goals by Areas of Your Life

The first thing to take into consideration when beginning to set your goals is that as a student-athlete, your time will be stretched to the max. The demands on you will be much different and much more challenging than those of the student body in general. Therefore, I suggest viewing your life and setting goals in three distinct categories—athletics, education, and social activity. Determine where you want to be in each area at the end of your college career and begin to work toward putting yourself there. I will use my goals to give you an example.

I decided early on in college that it was very important for me to (1) bring maximum effort and preparation to every workout, practice, and game; (2) achieve a grade point average that would put me on the Atlantic Coast

Conference Academic Honor Roll; and (3) make as many lasting friendships as possible. Setting these goals took an understanding of my abilities, the situation at hand, and a general idea of my plans after college. Now, you will notice that I didn't strive to be an all-American, valedictorian, and class president. You need to set goals that you control and that will force you to extend yourself. At the same time, don't set unrealistic goals or goals that are really only desires. Doing so will only set you up for failure, and that will hurt your confidence if these goals are not achieved.

Once the goals were set, my college life had focus. I didn't have to carry a piece of paper that said, "Work hard in the weight room, do my school work, and spend time with my friends." Because of the burning desire and consuming presence of my goals, I wouldn't even consider missing a workout or missing a homework assignment or leaving a friend in a lurch if I had the ability to help. Even a decision about going out with the guys versus staying at home alone and watching TV fell into my goal structure. Since I valued having lifelong friendships and had set this as a goal, I would normally opt to go with my friends. I recognized that a night on the town with my buddies was an opportunity to add to the "bond" I was striving to have in my friendships. Had getting into medical school been a priority, I may have acted a bit differently. This kind of thought process is what will allow you to achieve your goals. It will also help take the sting out of the many sacrifices you will be forced to make.

Clarity of goals and a strong vision makes decision-making much simpler.

Because my goal structure was firmly in place, I didn't mind the morning workouts, running in the heat of summer, or the late nights studying as much as many of my teammates did. I viewed these activities as the necessary ingredients in my quest for achievement. Proper goal setting provided the focus needed to reach my vision. You can do it too.

One thing to be aware of is not to set goals based on another person's standards. For example, being an all-conference selection is out of your hands because those accolades are often given for political reasons. Try to focus only on things that you can control. Rather than trying to be an all-conference performer, focus instead on beating your own personal record. In doing so, you assume complete responsibility for the accomplishment of your goals. If being all-conference is meant to happen, it will. If not, you can still have the satisfaction of meeting your own personal agenda.

Goal achievement is the result of planning. These old adages say it best:

- Proper prior planning prevents poor performance.
- Failing to prepare is preparing to fail.
- If you can imagine it, you can attain it.

Set your goals, set your plan, and set-up a strategy to be the success you are capable of becoming. Stop and take a minute to jot down some of your academic, athletic, and personal goals for your time in college. Remember to be specific. You can refine them over time, and you should certainly repeat the exercise once you've determined what career you want to pursue (more on that in chapter 4). Be sure to pay attention to whether or not they are really goals or just desires. Also be sure to set goals that will truly push you to be your absolute best. Your potential is unlimited, so don't limit yourself with low expectations. Set your goals high and work hard to accomplish each and every one of them. And make sure each one is SMART, including a time line.

Visualize Your Goals

Another important technique I use in goal achievement is placing visual reminders of my goals in the places I spend the most time. A visual reminder doesn't necessarily mean carrying around a piece of paper with your goals written on them. A simple, repeated visual representation becomes a subliminal message speaking directly to your subconscious mind. Once the goal is embedded in your subconscious, it becomes your default setting for decision-making. On top of that, the visual cue is a constant reminder to your conscious mind. And now your mind is a well-functioning team working from the same playbook.

From the time I was twelve years old, after I got cut by the soccer team, I had "no pain no gain" on my ceiling. I looked at it every night.

Some ideas for visualizing your goals include keeping a poster of the city you aspire to live in after graduation on your dorm room wall, listing quick snippets of your goals in your daily planner, leaving sticky notes for yourself in key places, or making your phone's lock screen image a picture of your role model. These reminders provide ongoing reinforcement of what you should be spending your time doing in order to accomplish your mission. Take a moment to write down how you will visually represent your goals.

📋 Build Your Game Plan

Academic Goals

1.

2.

3.

Athletic Goals

1.

2.

3.

Personal Goals

1.

2.

3.

What I Can Do to Visualize My Goals

1.

2.

3.

▶ Replay

The student-athlete experience has already prepared you for the methodical thought, planning, and action necessary to achieve your goals. Otherwise, you wouldn't be where you are, playing the sport you love at the college level. But perhaps your success so far was driven more by the goals your parents and coaches and teachers set for you. Now it's time to step up and set goals of your own. The keys to achieving your goals are to create SMART goals (reference page 24 as often as you need to), write them down, segment them by areas of your life, and visualize them. It also helps to have an accountability partner with whom you can discuss your goals and report your progress. Great mentors often make great accountability partners as well.

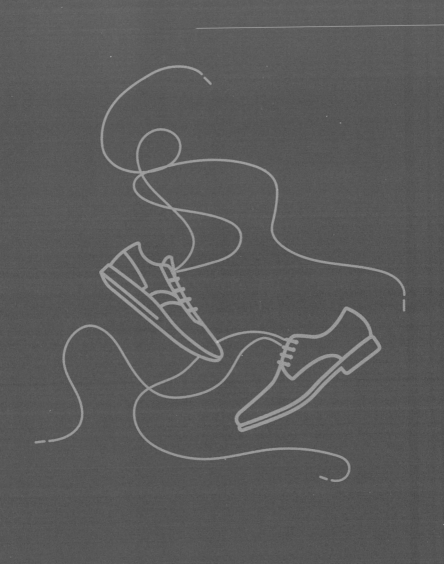

CHAPTER

3

Manage Your Time

"If only there were more hours in the day." I must have said that to myself on almost a daily basis over the course of my college career. With all that college had to offer, there never seemed to be enough time in the day to accomplish everything. That is why having priorities, which is done through both proper goal setting and time management, are critical to get the most out of every opportunity.

But how does one manage something that can't be changed? There is no way to stop the passing of time, stretch an hour into ninety minutes, or squeeze an extra hour into a day. The secret is utilizing the time you have to its full capacity. This means making choices. What kind of choices are you making with how you spend your time? Are you investing your time in activities that are essential to achieving your mission, or are you wasting it on video games, text messaging, Snapchat, Instagram, and other mindless pursuits?

I'm not a complete bump on a log. It's fine to goof around. What I've found is that goofing around is infinitely more pleasurable *after* you've taken care of business. You'll enjoy that movie or that video game more once you've written the paper and finished your workout.

Effective time management starts with clear goal setting (per the previous chapter). You must always keep your eye on the prize. Those who don't are prone to waste valuable time on worthless endeavors. Time is best viewed as a limited resource. If you equate it as such, you will be more inclined to use it wisely. I try to spend my time like I spend my money. In doing so, I get the most value out of every dollar and every minute. Start your time-management program by setting up an "hour budget."

First, get yourself a functional daily planner. My planner was the bible by which I lived throughout college. A good daily planner breaks each day up into hourly segments. It also has space for a "things to do" list and monthly calendars for the entire year. You can either use a digital planner or a paper planner—either will work—so use the one that you are most comfortable using.

If you don't currently use a calendar, then I suggest starting with the one already loaded on your smartphone. It's simple, free, and all of your data is automatically backed-up on the cloud. You can also sync your calendar with your tablet or laptop, giving you constant access to your information. Once you start using your daily planner effectively, you will want it with you at all times.

Map Your Days

Armed with the proper tool, you can begin to "map" your life more effectively than ever before. Start by plotting the dates of major events that will shape your life for the next year. You should take the schedule of your sports season and mark on your calendar the time and location of every event. Also note the starting date for preseason practice, the playoff schedule (the power of positive thinking), and the date of your team banquet.

You also need to include on your calendar the things you do every day, such as meals, study hall, etc. Just because you do these activities as part of your "routine" they need to be on your calendar, so you see how these events influence your available time to do other things. If you have the same activity every weekday at the same time, breakfast for example, you can set this up as a "recurring" event on your Google Calendar or iCal.

Other occasions worth noting from the start are the birthdays of friends and family, graduation dates, a planned road trip, the first and last day of classes, fall break, spring break, your schedule for midterms and finals, deadlines for class registration, rent payments, visits from friends or family, and trips home. The point I am trying to emphasize is that it's important to do long-term planning. As soon as you know of a date, put it down on your calendar.

If you need to do something on a certain day but not at a certain time on that day, you can put it on your calendar as an event for that day, just not at a specific time. This activity is now on your daily to-do list so that you can complete the task when you have a window of free time during the course of your day.

Proper planning and use of your calendar provide the structure and organization upon which to build your life-goal achievement strategy. Tony Robbins, a world-famous motivational speaker says, "If your life is worth living, it is worth recording." Your daily planner will serve as that record. It will also allow you to recognize potential conflicts long before they happen and prevent you from scheduling too much at one time.

After you plot your dates for the year, you can begin to focus more closely on the short-term agenda. Start by planning the very next day. You should note the time you are waking up, your class and practice schedule, meal times, study hall, and social activities. In doing so, you have created a snap shot of what you can expect tomorrow. This will have an influence on how you spend your time tonight. If the next day's schedule includes a three-hour practice and a major exam, you might want to think about putting this book away and getting some rest. However, if tomorrow is the first Saturday in two months that you can sleep in, put down this book and go have some fun!

Typically, I did my planning on Sunday evenings. I would note all my planned activities for the following week. This included blocking off my entire class and practice schedule, noting any meetings or functions I had to attend, and writing myself daily reminders under my "things to do list" for a particular day. Often, I would look at the next week and find events had already been planned. A month or possibly even six months earlier I may have scheduled something for that particular Wednesday.

Having a daily to-do list is of particular importance. This is something to compile and review every night. Having a list allows me to remember everything I must accomplish the next day. I note who I need to call, what I need to buy at the store, and what contact I need to make within my network. I check the list periodically throughout the day and cross-off chores once they have been completed. Those items I didn't get to are moved to the following day's list.

As you become more comfortable with using your daily planner, you can begin using it in conjunction with your goal-achievement program. I told you earlier that my main goals for college were to (1) bring maximum effort and preparation to every workout, practice, and game; (2) achieve a grade point average that would put me on the Atlantic Coast Conference Academic Honor Roll; and (3) make as many lasting friendships as possible. I accomplished all three by making the best use of my time.

Here's an example: Since I was not blessed with great speed or strength, I knew I had to be smarter than my competition in order to succeed. It was for this reason that I spent countless hours watching game films of our next opponent. Bringing maximum preparation to every game was a goal I had a burning desire to achieve, and thus I was willing to make the necessary sacrifices. Often, this sacrifice for me was the luxury of sleeping late (late being 8 a.m.). If upon my nightly review of the following day's itinerary I realized my schedule would not permit me to watch game film directly before my team meeting, I would adjust accordingly and watch the film early in the morning. In this case and in many others, goal setting and proper time management worked hand in hand in helping me achieve my goals.

In your daily planning, make sure you are devoting enough time toward the steps necessary to reach your goals. If your goal is to hit thirty home runs next season, evaluate what you need to do on a daily basis in order to accomplish it. If lifting weights is the answer, write it into your weekly schedule. Once it has been noted, you will be less likely to plan other activities during that part of your day.

Your daily planner also will serve as an excellent tool for analyzing why you fail. If your goal is to get all As and Bs and you fail a test, go back through your planner and note how much time you actually studied for the test. Chances are you didn't plan enough study time. In order to do better next time, note the date of the next exam on your calendar and set

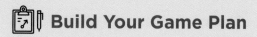 Build Your Game Plan

Plan your day tomorrow. The early bird catches the worm.

5 AM	
6 AM	
7 AM	
8 AM	
9 AM	
10 AM	
11 AM	
12 PM	
1 PM	

2 PM	
3 PM	
4 PM	
5 PM	
6 PM	
7 PM	
8 PM	
9 PM	
10 PM	

You should be resting by this point!

aside time in your schedule to devote to studying for it. We all have setbacks. How you respond to those setbacks is the mark of a true champion. Be proactive and allow more time to better prepare for the next obstacle. Careful planning will allow you to do just that!

Get started right away on improving your time management skills! Take a few minutes, right now, to plan your day tomorrow. Be sure to include time for meals, social events, free time, and all your academic and athletic obligations. Now, stop and ask yourself, are you getting the most out of every minute? If you're not on track, make the necessary changes immediately! If you need help with using an electronic calendar, find the help you need.

Here are some questions you can ask to make sure you are using your time most effectively:

- Are my athletic and academic obligations a priority?
- What am I doing each day to help achieve my goals?
- What, if any, adjustments do I need to make?

Focus on the Important Not "Urgent" Activities

In his book *The 7 Habits of Highly Effective People*, Stephen Covey advises us to divide a piece of paper into four quadrants labeled urgent or not urgent across the top and important or not important on the side. Then classify your activities or tasks according to these quadrants.

For most people, the (seemingly) urgent but not important things get in the way of the not urgent but still important things. The simple way to deal with that is to take care of business first with the important things. I call these nonurgent but nonnegotiable. Taking care of business first doesn't mean doing the important things at the crack of dawn; it means allocating time *any* part of the day and making that time sacred and nonnegotiable.

📋 Build Your Game Plan

Write down activities or items from your to-do list in the appropriate box to help you prioritize.

	URGENT	NOT URGENT
IMPORTANT		
NOT IMPORTANT		

This habit that I started in college has stayed with me as a parent. I thought I was busy then; then I had two kids! I'm an early bird, so I'm able to work out, stretch, and meditate before the kids are out of bed. I'm energized for "daddy time" in the morning since I've taken care of three of my nonurgent nonnegotiables (health, family, and prayer) before I leave.

My friend Tia, a runner in college, doesn't start to do her design work until after her kids are asleep and tends to be most creative around midnight. My friend Reggie, a college lacrosse player, lives in an apartment with thin walls, so he goes home on his lunch break and jams on his drums. Keep in mind that playing the drums is important to him. Winners in life make the time to do the things they love. Losers are on autopilot and are reactive to the tasks that others give them.

For all the excuses out there that impede us, there are often some legitimate objections. Your reality while in season is that you don't have enough hours in the day. That's why it's crucial to figure out what's nonnegotiable. I call it "Keeping the Main Thing the Main Thing."

Start by figuring out what's most important to you, your Main Thing. Then write it down. When you know what's nonnegotiable, your focus will narrow, and you accomplish your most important goals.

 **Replay**

Time is the most valuable thing you possess. Spend it wisely. Proper planning and determining your Main Things will help you do so.

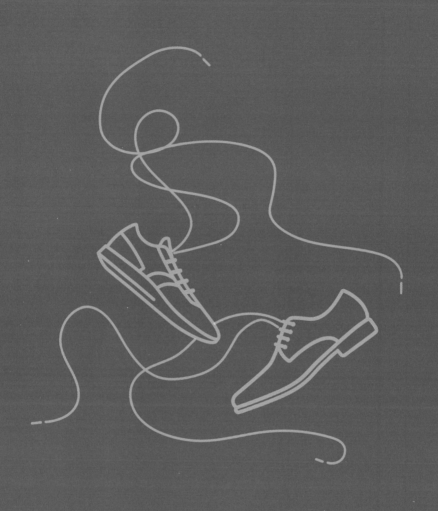

Network to Get Work

"It's not what you know; it's who you know." So goes the old adage. There is truth in it, but it doesn't tell the entire story. In some cases, the people we know don't know us back. Or they may know us, but that doesn't mean they are willing to help us. What's important in relationships is *how* someone knows you, not *if* they know you. In the real world, and in order to have real value, you must have relationships with people who like, trust, and respect you, are in a position to help you, and are *willing* to help you.

Today's job market is very competitive. Plenty of people with graduate degrees are unable to find work. It is crucial for you to use your current position as a college athlete to open up the door to summer internships and full-time jobs after graduation. For career discovery, internships, and job seeking, not to mention thriving in all aspects of life, you must understand that Facebook "friends" are worthless, but meaningful relationships are priceless.

Fortunately for you, the exposure of college athletics has never been greater. Whether you are a star on the football team or a role player in a non-revenue sport, a lot of people know who you are. More importantly, the people who know you as an athlete would welcome the opportunity to assist you in any way they can. The group of people I am referring to includes your teammates, your teammates' parents, professors, school administrators, reporters, classmates, alumni, and fans. One glance in the stands will give you an indication of the numerous resources you have. It is essential that you leverage this network to your advantage.

A great example is Rick Kramer. During my junior year, I met him at a scholarship donor banquet. The athletic department held the event on behalf of all the student-athletes on campus. The purpose was to honor academic achievement and to show appreciation to the many loyal supporters who had granted scholarships. Mr. Kramer, a scholarship donor, sought me out after learning that we were from the same town. We had an immediate connection. Mr. Kramer was very interested in me not only as an athlete but also as a person. We spoke briefly, and Mr. Kramer gave me his business card. I decided to write him the next day. Back then, email wasn't an option. Although there are times when an email or a message on LinkedIn may be appropriate, because people are overwhelmed with email, a handwritten note stands out even more today. (See more about "power notes" in chapter 5.)

The note was very simple, and the results were overwhelming. All I said to Mr. Kramer was how much I enjoyed meeting him and how nice it was to "have a fan in my corner" back home. Upon receiving the note, Mr. Kramer called me immediately. "Andy, this is Mr. Kramer. I just got your note, and you are one fine young man." The reaction from my little note was more than I could have ever imagined. I had no hidden agenda in writing Mr. Kramer. I wrote only to show appreciation for his support. What I learned from this encounter has been inspirational in my view of college athletics and one of the driving forces behind writing this book. Mr. Kramer and I agreed to get together at the beginning of the summer. After getting to know each other better and finding we had a lot in common (both of us are salesmen at heart), Mr. Kramer asked me if I had any interest in a summer job. Within six weeks of my first encounter with Mr. Kramer, he had me enrolled in a sales training seminar. This gave me the opportunity to sell corporate communication services in the Chapel Hill area during my free time at summer school. What an experience that turned out to be! At my sales training seminar, I met a number of influential people with whom I am still in contact today. I also learned a tremendous amount about salesmanship as a career and built a strong friendship with Mr. Kramer that has lasted over twenty-five years.

Get in the Game

One key to building a strong network is being aware of your environment and seizing your opportunities. Case in point is the night I met Mr. Kramer. While I was taking the time to talk with the scholarship donors, most of the other athletes were busy chatting amongst themselves. They all had the same opportunity to meet powerful members of the Tar Heel alumni network, yet few of them recognized the benefit of doing so. Why not at least introduce yourself to people who have a true love of your university's athletic department and the money to grant a scholarship?

Perhaps most of the student-athletes around me did not realize the willingness of these people to help, or they were intimidated with the idea of making the initial contact.

Maybe my classmates thought the future was too far off to worry about building those kinds of relationships. Whatever the reasons, they did not do it. They missed a chance to better position themselves for the future. Don't be a wallflower. Be assertive and act like a leader. Introduce yourself to people whenever possible and be quick to make new friends.

Depending on the size of the school you attend, there are hundreds or even hundreds of thousands of people who would love to meet you and help you in any way they can. Your job is to meet them and convert introductions into meaningful relationships.

My story may sound like finding the right career is easy. You might even say I was lucky. But Mr. Kramer didn't come looking for me in my dorm room, and he didn't contact me first after we met. I had to take the initiative to attend the scholarship banquet. I had to make the effort to meet the scholarship donors at the banquet instead of just hanging out with my friends. And I had to be proactive in following up quickly with Mr. Kramer after we met. In order to create my so-called luck, I had to be in the game, and I had to play aggressively.

What about you? Are you in the game? Do you know what you'd love to do for a career? Do you have strong relationships with people in the professional world who would be willing to help you find a job? Would you like a simple and effective plan to help figure all of this stuff out? Well you're in luck. I've combined my own personal experiences with the experiences of dozens and dozens of professionals to create a career launch formula. Your goal is three-fold: discover your passion, build your database of professional contacts, and turn those contacts into meaningful relationships. Here's how it works.

Career Launch Formula

❶	❷	❸	❹	❺
Meet with a broad range of professionals and ask them the basic discovery questions.	Perform internships and have "days in the field" to determine your professional passion.	Have deeper discovery meetings and seek more internships in your chosen field.	Follow up with every professional you meet to keep top-of-mind awareness.	Use the relationships you've built to launch your dream career.

A great example of this system in practice is when my friend Larry Farber asked me to take a meeting with his son Adam. Adam was a rising senior at the University of South Carolina, and he wanted a career in commercial real estate after graduation. I was extremely impressed with how Adam conducted himself at our meeting and was even more impressed with his ongoing follow-up throughout the following school year. It came as no surprise when I learned that Adam had achieved his goal of getting a job as a commercial real estate broker. Adam understood the importance of converting the introductions his father made for him into longstanding relationships. I asked Adam about his pre-graduation professional networking experiences, and he shared his step-by-step plan with me

The goal of Adam's follow-up plan was to establish credibility and keep top-of-mind awareness (TOMA). And he was successful in doing so. One of his discovery meetings led to a summer internship, and that internship led to a full-time job. Some of the most interesting things Adam shared with me about the process were:

- In almost every instance the professionals he met with were receptive to helping, and they liked

talking about themselves. Some even allowed him to
go on ride-alongs.

- Persistence pays off and in some cases is expected. If
you want a meeting, don't quit until you get it.
- Every time he had a discovery meeting, he got better
and more comfortable in dealing with professionals.
Practice really does make perfect.
- Don't be shy about asking your family for help. He
told me, "Pride won't pay the bills. My family helped
me open doors, but I got the job based on who I am."
- He wished he had started networking even earlier in
his college career.
- The people he was meeting with were also
researching him, and he needed to make sure his
web presence made a positive impression. What
would I learn about you if I did some research?
Make sure your online presence accurately portrays
how you want potential employers to see you.
And by the way, don't have a foolish email address
like partyhardy@gmail.com.

I've integrated Adam's plan with my own experience
in the guide below. Follow it to ensure a positive first
impression and ongoing relationships.

Set Up Discovery Meetings

The first step is to introduce yourself to working
professionals and talk with them about their work
during face-to-face "discovery meetings." The meeting
themselves are simple and should be a lot of fun. The
part that will require some work is *getting the meetings*.
The best way to get someone to agree to meet with you
is by having someone refer you to them. To find "warm
introductions" to professionals, start with the people who

care the most about your future—your family. Here's how the conversation should go: "Mom/Dad, I've decided to find out what I'd really love to do as a profession, so I can best position myself to have a fulfilling, profitable career. I want to interview successful people and ask them about the details of their careers. I'm hoping if I do ten or twenty of these interviews, I'll discover what I love and what I'd be best suited to do. Will you help me get appointments with some of your successful friends?" Mom and Dad want you off their payroll, so let them help.

Next, reach out to those who are most passionate about your sports program and are already following your career. They will surprise you with the knowledge they have about your accomplishments and background. These are the people who would be happy to help you, and it is your job to meet them. Here's how you find your way to these people:

- Ask your coach who from your area is most supportive of the program.
- Establish a relationship with the donor development department on your campus and ask them for the names of donors who would be willing to meet with you for career advice.
- Ask your teammates and classmates what their parents do for a living.
- Let your professors know that you want to build relationships with people already in the workforce in order to discover your passion and see if they have any ideas.
- Ask other relatives besides your parents if they would be willing to make introductions.
- Ask your high school coaches, teachers, teammates, and friends for ideas on who you can contact.

If circumstances are such that your current network isn't able to help with introductions, here are some other ways you can find your way to professionals:

- Attend campus events that include alumni.
- Attend career fairs on and off campus.
- Join local civic organizations or volunteer at a nonprofit.
- See if your local chamber of commerce has a young professionals' group or programs for college students to get involved.
- Attend any event that will put you in contact with professionals.

I urge you to proactively seek out people who can and would be willing to help you get ahead in different areas of your life. Start your list now below and use a separate sheet of paper or the downloadable playbook at goingproinlife.com/gameplan to record others.

Once you have your list, immediately start to schedule face-to-face meetings, even if those meetings need to be scheduled in advance based on your school vacation schedule. I suggest sending a simple email with an effective subject line. Below is an example you can tweak to fit your situation:

Subject Line: Mr. Harvey Rudolph of State U. suggested I contact you

Dear Ms. Smith,

My history professor, Mr. Rudolph, suggested I contact you about scheduling a meeting. I'm a sophomore on the _____ team, majoring in _____. I'm interested in learning more about what you

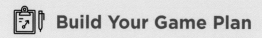

Build Your Game Plan

People to ask for warm introductions:

Name	Phone Number	Email Address

People to contact for discovery meetings:

Name	Phone Number	Email Address

*do so that I can better determine what sort of career
I should pursue. I'm available next week when I will
be home for spring break. Please let me know a good
time to call you to set up an in-person meeting.*

*Kind regards,
Betsy Jones*

The question of when to start having these discovery
meetings and how many to have is a personal decision,
but my advice is to start having them as a freshman with
the goal having two per month for the next four years.
Can you imagine the benefit of having 100 professional
contacts before you begin looking for a job, especially in
a job market that is tougher than ever? Taking the time to
figure out what you'd love to do for your profession will
put you ahead of 99 percent of the college population. Once
you discover the career you'd like to pursue, continue the
process with professionals in your chosen field.

Do Your Research and Prepare Your Questions
Once the meeting is scheduled, the next step is to research
the people you will be seeing and prepare the questions
you'd like to ask. Your goal is to answer the following
basic discovery questions to help you determine your career
path (save the last three for when you like the sound of the
first three):
- What does the business or industry do?
- What does the person spend their time doing on a
  day-to-day (hour-by-hour) basis?
- What do they like and dislike about their job?
- What do they suggest you do to begin a career in
  that field?

- Would they be willing to let you spend a day "on the job" with them?
- Would they be willing to introduce you to others who might be helpful?

By taking time to learn about the person you will be engaging, you will be better prepared to find your answers and make a great first impression. Nothing will make you sound smarter and more prepared than referencing information from your research about the company, industry, or person during your meeting.

Google them and review their company website. Learn what the company does, who their customers are, where they have locations, and if they are advertising any job positions they are trying to fill. Also uncover any mission statements or slogans they use.

Research both the person and the company on social media. Start with LinkedIn and Facebook. See if you can come up with some personal information such as the number and age of their kids, their hobbies, or what they like to do in their free time.

Copy any articles or information you find and bring them with you. When they see that you've taken the time to research them, it will demonstrate that you take the meeting seriously. More importantly, devise some questions based on the information you've uncovered. For example:

- Ms. Smith, I see that your first job out of college was with Acme Industries. How did you find that job, and what did the experience of working for Acme teach you?
- I saw on your Facebook page that you like country music. I do too. Who are some of your favorite performers?

- I learned that you have a child at Central College. How did they choose that school?

If you ask smart questions, people think you are smart. Use your research to craft engaging, open-ended questions that force the person to share even more information about themselves. But remember to never ask a question that your research could have answered for you.

These are some questions you must ask in all instances:

- How did you get into X or why did you choose X?
- Tell me more about yourself and what you do.
- What's your biggest goal?
- When you think about your goal, what is the biggest challenge?
- What didn't I ask that you'd like to share?

These are high-level, open-ended questions that allow plenty of space for the person you're meeting to answer in their most comfortable manner. They are also the sort of questions that, when you get an answer, should lead you to more good questions.

Show Respect to Get Respect

When the day of the meeting comes around, remember that to get respect, you must first give respect. This means showing up on time, dressing professionally, and taking notes during the meeting.

Remember to confirm the appointment via email the day before the meeting. This practice gives you a chance to show off professionalism, and it will reduce the amount of times you get stood up. Then get to the appointment on time. If you're going to be late, call the person and let them know. You may not think being five minutes late is a big deal, but to some people it is a sign of disrespect. By calling, you at least show respect for their valuable time.

Look the part. Being on time and enthusiastic is a good start, but that alone won't ensure a good first impression. Your appearance is important. Dirty fingernails, shirt stains, and scuffed shoes won't cut it. None of it goes unnoticed.

Turn-off your cell phone and be ready to stand up and shake their hand when they approach. Your time with a working professional is their time, not yours. Be respectful of that by never having cell phone distractions during a meeting.

"Lobby" for more information. Once on-site, make good use of your "lobby time." How do they answer the phone? What awards, mission statements, and company brochures are on display? Do they have a sign-in book? Who is coming to see them? The closer you look, the more insight you'll gain. Soak up all the information you can. This will make you seem more prepared and help the conversation flow.

Finally, you're in front of the person for that initial interaction. You look the part, you've done your research, and your confidence is high. Instead of using some cheesy opening like, "Is that a picture of your family?" or "Where did you catch that fish?" use the information you've uncovered to begin with a question or statement that builds respect and increases validity. Maybe it's a comment about a mutual acquaintance or perhaps a question concerning information on their website. Whatever it is, make sure it reflects your premeeting preparation. After you've broken the ice with some casual conversation, you can then start to ask the questions that you really want to have answered based on your preparation.

First impressions matter. Research reveals that it takes less than five seconds to make a negative impression. Once made, it takes a full six hours of positive interaction to make up for the initial feelings. Get it right the first time. The choice is yours—either make your impression memorable or be prepared to have meetings that don't produce positive results.

Be sure to take notes during each meeting. It's a great way to show respect, and the best way to remember all the good information you receive. I'm certain you will find that most people will be happy to answer these questions. I'm also certain that the more people with whom you speak, the better understanding you will have on what you might like to do as a career.

I met Noah Turner, a tight end on the UNC football team, when I spoke to the team about the importance of professional networking. Noah did a great job following up with me, and he asked if I had any professional contacts in the Chicago area, his hometown, who would be willing to meet with him during his summer break. I made an email introduction to my friend Vaughn Moore, a UNC alum and the CEO of an international logistics company, and a meeting was scheduled. Here's what Noah had to say after the meeting:

> *I took multiple things away from it, but the biggest was the need to write a detailed plan for my dream of owning a training facility. Not just telling people "I'm going to do this or that" but writing down an exact plan to accomplish that goal or vision. Along with the plan, I must make sure to always have a funding source, partially your own money and finding a trustworthy person to help you as well. Another thing I learned was that sometimes the path you always envisioned for yourself can change in an instant or change over time without you even noticing the change*

or the success you're having with the change. Another idea he told me was to always "be present." This quote came from Mr. Moore after I asked, "When you achieve so much success and wealth, how do you make sure to balance your personal life and family life?" Mr. Moore told me to always "be present" in what you're doing. If you're working, put all your energy into work; if you're with your family, give them all your focus. So whatever you're doing, always be present in that situation. Along with that, he talked a lot about manifestation, which I do a lot myself, envisioning success on the football field and post-football career. But hearing it from a very successful man helped reassure that I'm taking small steps toward the right direction. I also learned that building your personal brand is very important, whether it's through social media or in-person experiences. Last thing was to not limit myself to the Chicago area. Although it's your comfort zone, you never know what opportunities await you somewhere else.

As a result from meeting Mr. Moore, I plan to write out an entire business plan for my training facility, taking from my personal experiences, classes I take, and closely watching the positives and negatives of that industry. Also, figure out where that industry is underserved and take advantage of it. Mr. Moore also suggested taking accounting classes, finance classes, and a public speaking class to make sure I have a base knowledge of those skills and not to wait till after college to learn those skills. I really enjoyed this experience and plan to continue to make connections like this in the Chicago area and anywhere around the country to help me with my post-football career.

I plan to follow up with Mr. Moore by periodically keeping in touch with him and taking advantage of any connections he provides for me. Also, in the future I plan to ask Mr. Moore for guidance in the professional world, possibly through a job offer or his suggestions for a job.

The best outcome from this meeting is that I will find myself having a very successful post-football career. Mr. Moore and I shared a lot of common traits, proving to me, if he can do it, I can do it as well. I was in complete awe by his office, clothes, confidence, presentation, and love of the Tar Heels. I could've talked to him for hours because I too want to be in the same position as him at some point in my life.

It motivated me, inspired me, and helped create a vision in my mind I would have never seen if not for this meeting. It was an experience out of my comfort zone, but one that has changed a lot of perspectives on my life.

Follow Up to Build Meaningful Relationships

After each discovery meeting, your job is to convert those connections into bona fide relationships. You will call on these relationships when you are preparing to graduate and to find a job, so your job is to create depth and meaning in your relationships now, before you need anything from them.

So what does it mean to have depth in your professional relationships? Let's think about it in terms of your favorite social media platform. Do you have at least 100 friends there? How about 500? 1,000? How strong would you say these relationships are? Would they be willing to lend you a hand if you needed help in the middle of the night? In most cases, it's highly unlikely. In reality, you should consider yourself very fortunate if you have even a few friends who could be counted on 24/7.

In short, the saying "it's not what you know, it's who you know," is really a bunch of baloney. Simply knowing someone doesn't mean they'd help. I've learned that it's about "how" you know someone and, most importantly, "how" they feel about you. Do they like you; do they trust you; do they respect you? If they do, they *might* help. Your job is to make the people you meet come to like, trust, and respect you, and a follow-up plan can help achieve that goal.

A critical part of the plan is to follow-up very quickly. Money loves speed! Immediately after each meeting, send a handwritten thank-you note. We'll talk more about power notes and personal branding in the coming chapters, but I'll mention here that if you don't have personalized stationery, get some, or use stationery that identifies your school.

Also send an email that includes all of your contact information and links to all your social media platforms. And of course, send them invitations on all of their social media outlets, especially LinkedIn. If you don't already have a LinkedIn account, it is imperative that you create one and that you provide as much content about yourself as possible. You can check me out on LinkedIn for an example of how to present yourself and your athletic experience in a compelling manner.

When you make promises during your meeting, keep those promises. It may be forwarding them an article that you discussed or arranging a sideline pass for their kids. Do what you say you are going to do, just like you would for a friend. I've found that the best way to *have* a friend is to *be* a friend, and you need more professional friends!

You also need to create an electronic database that includes all the contact information of all the people you meet. If you don't currently have a method to store contact information, start with something as simple as Google Contacts, a free service that is part of Gmail.

Create Ongoing TOMA (Top-of-Mind Awareness)

Because you've successfully connected with your new relationships on social media and you have their email addresses in your database, you are well prepared to start using technology to strengthen the bonds.

I want you to focus your digital media efforts on providing "insiders" access to your life as a college student-athlete by sending ongoing email updates and postings on social media that include things like images

 Build Your Game Plan

Discovery Meeting Checklist

Name	Phone	Email	Date of Appointment

and videos of your locker room and visitors' locker rooms, interviews of your teammates and coaches, and pregame selfies. Use your imagination to create fun, engaging content that shows your personal brand positively and professionally, gives a behind-the-scenes peek into your sports world, and makes people want to learn more about you.

Your life as a college student is fascinating to people in the workforce, and because you also play sports, their interest is even stronger. By creating digital content that professionally showcases your talents and sharing that content with as many people as possible via social media and direct e-mailing, you are leveraging technology to strengthen relationships. It's where high-tech meets high-touch!

Email Confirmation #1 Sent	Email Confirmation #2 Sent	Research Complete	Thank-You Note Sent	Contact Added to Database	Connected on LinkedIn	Connected on Insta/Facebook

"But, Andy," you're thinking, "This is a lot of work."
OK, it will take some work. But you know what's even
tougher? *Unemployment.* If you can really hone in on
making relationships that will help you learn what you
love, nothing I'm asking you to do will seem like work.
Plus, the effort I'm asking you to make is for a relatively
short period of time, just like an airplane at takeoff.

Hone Your Conversation Skills

The most important skill you can master to get the
most out of the Network to Get Work plan is your ability
to communicate clearly and be "likeable," in other words,
to be a good conversationalist. The good news is you can
learn this skill. You can learn to think quickly on your feet,
how to be funny, and how to quickly establish rapport
with people. You can learn to be likeable. Here are some
resources to help you improve in these areas:

- Join your local Toastmasters club.
- Take a public-speaking course.
- Take an improv class.
- Read Dale Carnegie's book *How to Win Friends and Influence People.*

Take as many classes as possible that will hone these
skills. Check out the drama and journalism departments at
your school for more opportunities to speak or perform in
front of a group or on camera. Your ability to communicate
with others and to make a compelling presentation, will
benefit you greatly.

▶ Replay

Networking is the lifeblood of the professional world. It's how people make meaningful connections to establish mutually beneficial relationships. And it's a numbers game: the more connections you make, the higher the chances of finding your people. As a student-athlete, you have access to an incredible network of supporters. Follow the Network to Get Work plan to take advantage of the connections available to you in this pivotal moment in your life.

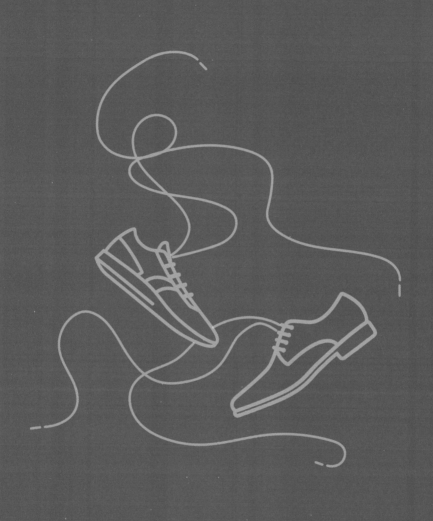

CHAPTER

5

Write Power Notes to Power Relationships

Are you tired of people complaining about younger generations? You could get defensive, or you could see it as an opportunity. (Notice how I've cultivated the habit of seeing everything in life as an opportunity).

Since society today is full of people with very poor manners—and many people have prejudged you based on your generational characteristics—simply saying "please" and "thank you" will get you a long way. Social etiquette has been diminishing for a while now. Whether it's texting while someone is talking to you or failing to look them in the eye, many people are flat-out rude. The key to getting ahead in life is to differentiate yourself from the crowd in a positive manner.

Follow Through

If saying "please" and "thank you" gets you rewarded, just think how much can be gained from a handwritten note of appreciation. Using what I call "power notes" has allowed me to set myself apart on many occasions. I call them power notes because of the powerful, positive feelings the recipient of the note gets from reading it. It is also because of the power you will receive from writing it. The note gives you the power that comes with respect. The recipient views you differently. Your positive qualities are recognized, and the recipient goes out of their way to help you in the future. Writing a power note is quick and easy. The results are unbelievable.

The story I told earlier about my note to Mr. Kramer is an excellent example of using power notes. A handwritten note shows a person that you care. The recipient knows that despite all you have to do in the course of a day, you took a few moments to sit down and acknowledge him or her in writing. Just think of the powerful message it conveys to that person. It says, "You're special to me, and I appreciate all that you do for me." As you begin to network and meet people, follow up your encounter with a quick note. Even if the contact you make with a person is only by phone, a power note is still appropriate.

Another example of how writing a follow-up note worked in my favor came after meeting a powerful UNC alumnus in Charlotte at an Educational Foundation meeting (UNC's athletic booster club). Here's what happened. I had not yet graduated, but since I had accepted a sales job in Charlotte, I made the two-hour drive from Chapel Hill to attend the meeting in hopes I could make some new friends in what would be my new home in a few months. Pat Crowley, a teammate of mine, came along with me.

Pat's dream of playing in the NFL was much more realistic than mine. He was a *Football News* all-American offensive guard and was named all-Atlantic Coast Conference three times. So why was he attending a networking event instead of dreaming about his multimillion-dollar football career? Because Pat was committed to going pro in life. And, like you, he wanted to give himself as many options as possible. Even if in the back of his mind Pat didn't think he'd be working a real job until *after* his NFL career, at age twenty-two he had the savvy to begin preparing for a life after football. He understood then what I'm doing my best to impart to you: being a college athlete creates unparalleled opportunities.

Being a college athlete creates unparalleled opportunities.

Our head football coach, Mack Brown, promised to introduce Pat and me to the crowd, so I knew it would be a great chance to start building a network in my new city. At the meeting, Pat and I met John Black, who was the manager of a securities firm in Charlotte and was very involved with Carolina athletics. John told us both that if he could be of assistance to either one of us, feel free to call him. Of course, Pat and I both followed up our meeting with a note thanking him for his kind offer and assuring him we would call.

Upon arriving to town, I got together with John. I don't know if it was my note that made the difference, but I do know that John was very receptive to getting together as he had promised. Since my first job was selling business telephone systems, he put me in touch with numerous people in town who have helped me to grow in my career. He also provided me with advice and insight that made my transition to a new city a lot easier. Many of these introductions turned into customers, friends, or advisors. From that one introduction to John, my professional life has been greatly enhanced.

As for Pat, things didn't go as planned. He tore his knee during training camp with the New England Patriots. No NFL contract. And guess what? Pat still went pro! Pat's follow-up with John proved to be very rewarding as well. Just days after Pat's NFL dream was dashed, John offered him a job. Pat Crowley never got to block for Tom Brady, but he has been gainfully employed as a stockbroker for nearly thirty years—all because of a power note!

This story is a perfect application of everything I want you to learn. Pat and I used our positioning as college athletes to meet an alumnus who cared about us because we were athletes. We followed up our meeting with a note to gain his respect and friendship. If you want to go pro, do the same thing for yourself. The results are worth the small amount of effort.

Power notes are important not only in the networking I suggest you do as a college student-athlete but also as a general member of society. Look for ways to thank people. For instance, before I graduated, I wrote thank-you notes to my academic advisors, a number of professors, and some of my coaches. I even wrote to some of my competitors.

Today, as a salesman, I write notes to my customers all the time. Even after an appointment where the sale is going to be small, I still follow up within a day by writing to thank them for their time at our last appointment. When somebody tells me they bought my service because of my thoughtful follow-up, it feels almost as good as being the lead blocker for a touchdown run. Most of that follow-up refers to my notes, so I know they are working.

Side note: never walk into someone's house empty-handed. My mom nagged me incessantly about this as a kid. Now I can't thank her enough. If someone is kind enough to host you at their home or cook you a meal (such as your roommate's parents), show appreciation. Ten dollars on flowers or a dessert is all it takes to distinguish yourself. People think athletes are entitled and younger generations lack social skills. What does that mean for you? Say it with me now: OPPORTUNITY! It's easy to stand out in a crowd when others are unwilling to go the extra mile.

Writing power notes is a great habit to form. Write your friends' parents to thank them after sleeping at their home. Acknowledge your favorite teachers at the end of the semester. Drop your high school coaches a note to let them know how special they are to you. You will be amazed at the powerful effect writing these notes can have on your life. I have been in touch with my high school football coach since I graduated. It turns out his daughter lives in Charlotte, and because of my ongoing relationship with my coach, I've been friends with her for twenty-five years. Her friendship and guidance have been an enriching part of my life, and it came as the result of always staying in touch with my high school coach, mostly by sending notes.

Who in your life has made a positive difference? Have you taken time to let them know your appreciation? There is no better time than now.

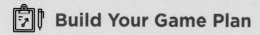

Build Your Game Plan

Create a list of those you would like to acknowledge and begin writing them notes as soon as possible.

1.
2.
3.
4.
5.
6.
7.
8.
9
10.
11.
12.
13.
14.
15.
16.
17.
18.
19.
20.

▶ Replay

In the digital era, handwritten notes and old-fashioned courtesy stand out. And it's so easy to do. Say "please" and "thank you," do what you say you will do, and send power notes to show your appreciation.

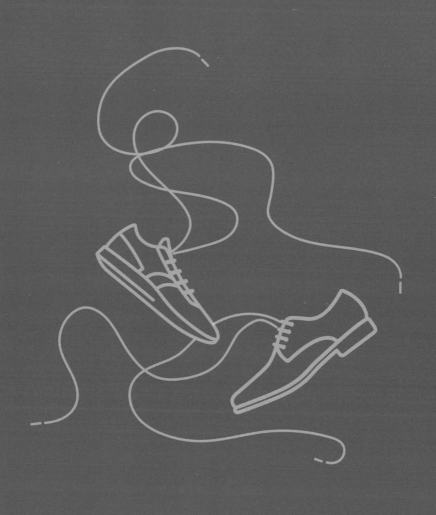

Create Your
Personal Brand

A brand is a promise. Think of iconic brands like Nike, Apple, and Tiffany. Those brands promise a certain type of experience or level of value and bring to mind certain images. Michael Jordan defying gravity. FaceTiming with loved ones across the country. Flawless diamonds in a little, blue box. Your job is to create positive images when you come to mind. Power notes are a great way to build a positive brand for yourself, but they are just the start.

Just as you will research the people you meet, they will also research you. What they find is totally up to you. It's a very fine line between ordinary and memorable. That fine line is your opportunity. All you have to do is put your own unique twist on the ordinary, and you'll easily set yourself apart from the other job-seeking competition. How do you do that? By establishing yourself as a unique brand.

What promise is your brand making? You want it to stand for professionalism, creativity, and hard work. What images come to people's minds when they think about you? In this chapter, you will learn strategies to demonstrate how to create your brand. The minute people hear or see your name, they will instantly be thinking:

- Mover and shaker
- Up-and-coming young professional
- The type of person they want in the trenches with them

Most of your fellow job seekers will have a similar level of education, positive references, and meaningful life experiences. Granted, there may be a subtle twist here or there, but they're preaching the same stuff. So why then would a prospective employer choose to hire you? They won't unless you make a memorable impression.

Take a look at the list below and ask yourself how memorable (and positive) of an impression you are making on those who are exposed to you and your experience via each channel:

- Facebook
- Twitter
- Instagram
- LinkedIn
- Personal website or blog
- Personal email signature
- Personal email address
- Personal stationery
- Business card

Each time a potential employer, mentor, coworker, sponsor, booster, etc., is exposed to you via one of the above channels, it is an opportunity to create a value-added impression of yourself in their mind. To do this you must be funny, educational, unique, or all three. Here are some suggestions that will help you get it right:

- Pay for professional help. While a good website, social media presence, resume, or business card might cost you a few bucks, the results are well worth it.
- Show off your skills via third-party endorsements. If you say it about yourself, it's bragging, but if someone else says it about you, it's proof. Use LinkedIn's recommendations section to request endorsements from coaches, teachers, classmates, previous employers, and others as appropriate. Draw positive attention to yourself by putting those testimonials on every available platform.
- Use appropriate humor. Put a great meme on your Twitter profile. Post a "joke of the week" on your Facebook feed. Give a riddle on your voice mail greeting. You get the idea. But keep it clean to leave a positive impression with potential employers.
- Provide "insiders" access to your life as a college student-athlete.

Also remember that the people around you can also influence your brand inadvertently. You may have heard that you need to get rid of your toxic friends. Not only does it sound like a big ordeal, but also you're *focusing on toxicity*. For me, it was much more effective to figure out who I wanted to spend time with and make time for those people. Once I did that, there weren't enough hours left to spend with the people who didn't bring positive things into my life. I didn't have to put any energy into eliminating the toxic friends from my life; they just got squeezed out.

How can you come up with memorable ideas for improving your brand? It takes a clear mind, a positive environment, and the study of memorable people and things. Research your role models, determine what makes them memorable, and decide what traits you want to borrow from them.

Protect Your Public Image

What you do alone and behind closed doors is your business. What you do in public is the world's business, whether you like it or not. I like to call this the "front page test." Never say or do anything in front of other people or write anything to other people (including what you might assume are private text messages) that you wouldn't want to see on the front page of the *New York Times* the next day. Everyone has a video recorder, camera, and screenshot capabilities on them at all times in their smartphones. You have no control over what they do with that power. And if they post things online that conflict with the personal brand you're trying to establish, potential employers will likely see it.

A few cautionary tales come to mind. One that really hits hard is the time Fernando Bryant was fired from a coaching job at a Christian high school because of a three-year-old post on his wife's Instagram account. It depicted him and his wife standing together, and Bryant was holding a bottle of liquor. Bryant said the photo was for a sponsor at an event and that those who hired him were aware of the photo. But once he was on the job, a parent complained and questioned Bryant's Christian values. And that was it. Bryant was out. This case seems extreme and unfair, but it is unfortunately how the world works right now. The employer could have just as easily been a large corporation with shareholders to answer to instead of parents.

I should also caution you about drug use. I know conflicting laws across the country regarding marijuana

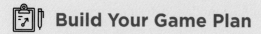 **Build Your Game Plan**

Write down five brands that you admire or identify with.

1.
2.
3.
4.
5.

What do they do that makes them memorable?

1.
2.
3.
4.
5.

How can you apply that to your own brand (you)?

1.
2.
3.
4.
5.

use can be confusing. Bottom line: marijuana possession is still a federal crime and still a crime in most states. Most employers will frown upon it as well. Other narcotics and "recreational drugs" are flat-out against the law no matter where you are. They could get you in major trouble and damage both your body and mind in a variety of ways. Besides avoiding drugs yourself, you should also be supportive of and find help for any friend or teammate you know has a problem with substance abuse. Pretending a problem doesn't exist is not a good solution.

▶ Replay

Your personal brand shows and tells employers what they can expect from you. You create your brand and reinforce it in how you show up in public and online. Determine what you want your brand to say about you and take proactive, intentional steps to establish and protect that brand. And if you haven't already joined LinkedIn, do so immediately and start building contacts.

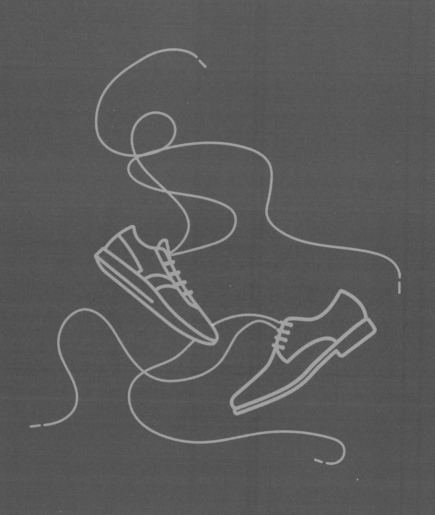

Land Your Dream Job

Fortunately, a lot of companies today make a big effort to hire college student-athletes. They have already discovered that people with a background in sports are able to better compete in the business world. Often, they have hired athletes from your campus before and would be receptive to doing so again. Use this to your advantage and try to interview with these firms. For those companies that have not yet recognized the benefits of hiring college athletes, it is up to you to educate them on just how well trained you are and what a great asset you would be for their company.

Ask yourself this question, "If I owned a company and had the ability to mold the perfect employee, what would he or she be like?" How about dedicated? Self-motivated? Determined? Resilient? Goal oriented? And wouldn't it be even better if this person were a well-educated leader and team player with a great work ethic, superior time-management skills, and the ability to make quick decisions under pressure? If this is the person you are looking for, take a good look in the mirror. College athletics teaches you all these skills and more!

You are better qualified to deal with the rigors of a forty-plus hour week based on your experiences as a student-athlete. On a daily basis, you must juggle a full class load, attend team meetings, participate in practice, maintain your academics, and try to have an active social life. In order to negotiate this rigorous schedule, you must be proficient in time management, have a great deal of dedication and determination, and also be self-motivated enough to stick with the program even when nobody is watching. Sports are the best teachers of teamwork and quick decision-making skills under pressure. They are the perfect training ground for learning all the skills necessary to compete in the workforce. Your job is to convey these skills to employers. This chapter is about how. Once you recognize the fact that you have these skills, the next step is learning how to market them to other people.

Create a Powerful Resume

The resume is the first line of defense that companies use in screening potential job candidates. Not having a good one could prevent you from even having the opportunity to get up to bat. Your school's career center may have a template you can use to start. If not, Microsoft Word has templates. Once you have a good draft resume, go back to the career center for a resume review.

The key elements to a great resume are using action verbs, highlighting accomplishments, and being specific about the value you add and how you believe that would contribute to your dream company's goals.

Be certain that everything you put on your resume focuses on your strengths and highlights the "soft skills" you have learned as a college student-athlete. Don't hesitate to clearly spell out what these skills are and how you learned them.

It may not be as obvious to the interviewer as it is to you. Sell your:

- Perseverance—you work for the win no matter what else is going on in your life.
- Resilience—when you fall down or lose, you get back up and keep working.
- Accountability—as part of a team, you understand your role and how to talk about it with your coaches and teammates.
- Communication—you can absorb, apply, and give constructive criticism, even when that critique means you need to push beyond your limits.
- Time-management—you expertly juggle various aspects of your life and work.

I also advocate the use of bullet points to hit on your main points. The people who prescreen your resume will often have a hundred or more to look at. They are not interested in reading about your life history. Therefore, you need to clearly and concisely list your highlighted qualifications and move on. Draw attention to what's most important and save the rest to talk about once you get the interview.

Become an Interview Superstar

In the "Network to Get Work" chapter, we covered how to make a good first impression and get the most out of your discovery meetings. Many of the same skills apply to interviewing for jobs.

Before you ever step foot in the interview room, do some research on the company. Nothing will make you sound smarter and more prepared than referencing information from your research about the company, industry, or person during your meeting. Most career placement offices have information on the companies that come to campus, so use that resource. At a minimum, know their products or services, the approximate size of the company, locations of offices, and some general history about the firm. This will show the interviewer that you care enough about the job to do your homework, and it will give you some information from which to derive some appropriate questions about the company when the time comes. And trust me, the time always comes! I like to ask at least two questions. Some examples could include: Why is this position open? What five words would you use to describe the culture of this team/department/office? Do you offer continuing education opportunities? Does this company tend to promote from within, or do they hire externally for upper-level management positions? But remember never to ask a question that your research could have answered for you.

Also give some thought to the potential questions you might be asked. Your prior interviewing experience should give you a good idea of what you can expect, but stay ready for anything. Be prepared with a number of events and examples from your academic, athletic, and personal lives to answer various questions that might come your way.

Another course of action I suggest is enrollment in a public speaking course. As a communication studies major, I found this class to be the most beneficial of any class I took in my college career. The ability to clearly present your ideas orally will be one of your greatest assets, not only in interviewing but also throughout your life. If you have not taken this course already, please do yourself a favor and enroll immediately.

The next thing you must do to become a superstar is to familiarize yourself with the general process of interviewing. This can be accomplished only with practice. Like anything else in life, the more you do something, the better and more comfortable you become. To get comfortable with interviewing, I suggest that initially you submit a resume to every company that comes to campus. This in turn will lead to a lot of interviewing opportunities. The repetition of interviewing will give you a chance to polish your skills and teach you about the wide variety of jobs that exist. Doing this gave me the training I needed to do well on the interviews that really counted.

You will also need to look the part. Being on time and enthusiastic is a good start, but that alone won't ensure a good first impression. If you don't care about your own appearance, the employer's perception will be that you don't care about your job or them either. Take and pass the mirror test before walking out the door. Pass the smell test as well. Shower, apply deodorant, brush your teeth, and avoid strong perfumes and colognes. You want to smell nice but not overpowering.

Mirror Test Checklist

☐ Your hair is clean and styled.
☐ You got a proper night's sleep, so your eyes are bright and alert.
☐ Your face is clean. If you're a man who sports a beard, your beard is well groomed.
☐ Your clothes are professional and clean.
☐ Your nails are clean and filed.
☐ Your shoes are clean and scuff free.

Once you are in front of the interviewer, be certain that you have your "interview game face" on. Be the most positive and enthusiastic person that the interviewer has spoken with all day. A positive attitude is like a magnet—people are drawn to it. Be confident and relaxed and, most importantly, keep a smile on your face.

Before going into an interview, I used to have a "pregame" ritual to pump myself up. Just like in sports, you have to be mentally prepared to perform at your peak level. I would always take a few minutes to fill my head with positive thoughts, review my answers to potential questions, and reflect back on my preparation up until this point. I always knew going in that I was the right person for the job. As a result of college athletics, I had conditioned myself to accomplish anything I set my mind to. Through the use of the superior communication skills I had learned, I was prepared to tell these people why, based on my past experiences and current skill level, I was their man. I was eager to answer any questions that came my way and relished the chance to ask targeted, thought-provoking questions about their company in return. Looking at the number of job offers I received, the preparation obviously paid off.

Once again, being different is better. This couldn't be more true than in the interview process. The typical interviewer speaks with hundreds of job applicants every year. One company I received an offer from, Gallo Wine, interviewed 2,500 people and made only thirty offers. They told me the biggest reason I received an offer was because of my background as a student-athlete and their perception that this experience would help me persevere when the job got difficult. They were impressed that I overcame a coaching change, position change, and injuries.

Since you have such limited time to make an impression, it is essential not to waste a second. Be prepared to talk about how the skills you built as a student-athlete will help you meet the requirements of the particular job you are interviewing for. In my case, I was interviewing for sales jobs. I knew that the skills necessary for success in sales

📋🖊 **Build Your Game Plan**

List five skills you've learned as a student athlete.

1.
2.
3.
4.
5.

How would you incorporate those skills into a resume in a way that will get you noticed?

1.
2.
3.
4.
5.

How will you describe those skills to the interviewer in a way that will help you in the job you're applying for?

1.
2.
3.
4.
5.

were the same skills that made me a success at football. One skill in particular is resiliency, the ability to bounce back after a defeat or letdown. In comparing my football experiences to what I anticipated in selling, I focused a lot on my ability to keep a positive attitude despite suffering through back-to-back one and ten seasons.

For example, an interviewer would ask, "Why are you so certain about your ability to continue to prospect for new customers after a potential client rejects your product?" My answer was, "Over the course of my college career, I was forced to deal with a lot of adversity and disappointment. For two years in a row, I devoted a large portion of my life to a football team that continued to lose almost every game. Just when I thought it couldn't get any worse, we'd lose again. Through it all, I continued to work hard on improving my own skills and assisted my teammates in keeping a positive attitude. As a result, I was an integral part of one of the greatest turnarounds in college football history. After two 1–10 seasons, I was a starter and leader on a team that went 6–4–1 and 7–4 the following seasons. From that experience, I learned that hard work and perseverance do pay off."

There are dozens of other examples like this one that I used to link the skills learned in college athletics to the skills necessary for success in the workplace. I am certain that anyone reading this book can make the same sort of applications. Whether you sit the bench for four years or you are an all-American, the skills you learn range far beyond anything that could ever be taught in a classroom setting. Have some examples in mind and use those experiences to set yourself apart from the rest. The result could be the job of a lifetime.

Rehearse your stories. You play the way you practice. The outline presented here for job seeking and interviewing success is one that worked well for me. In a very tight job environment, I was able to market the skills learned from college athletics well enough to have a number of job offers to choose from. As a student-athlete, you are special. Keep this in mind at all times and sell the advantages you have to those doing the hiring. Presenting yourself effectively can be very rewarding and very lucrative.

Follow Up on Every Interview

The final step in the job-seeking process is an appropriate follow up. Again, I think a polished, handwritten power note is the answer. Thank the interviewer for their time, reiterate why you think you are the right person for the job, and ensure them of your interest in the company. If a list of references was requested at the interview, now is the time to send that as well.

 **Replay**

Playing college-level sports has prepared you for the workforce in ways that few other experiences can. You will graduate with the soft skills employers are clamoring for. Now all you need to do is land the interview with a great resume and then nail it by being well prepared and telling your story in a compelling way.

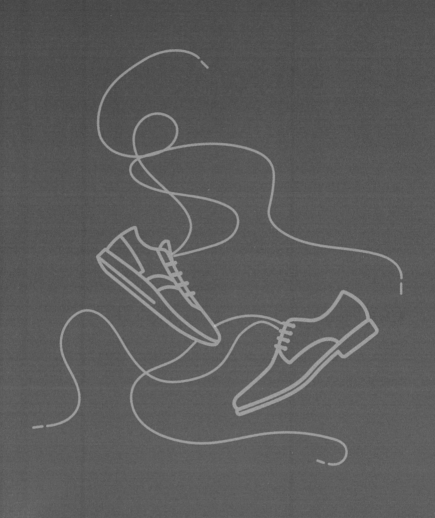

CHAPTER

8

Manage Your Attitude

Your current state of mind influences your perspective and outlook on the situation at hand. To me, perception is one of the most interesting concepts around. Think about how many times you perceived a situation completely opposite from the person you were with. Perhaps the other person thought your day at the beach was wonderful while you felt it was miserable. How could two people do the exact same thing yet have totally different opinions about what they did? The answer is simple: attitude.

Like goal setting, entire books are devoted to the power of positive thinking. What I'm interested in, however, is the role positive thinking plays in your life as a college student-athlete. In order to set the scene for this topic, I'll show the effect that negative thinking can have on you.

Whether we choose to admit it or not, everyone has occasional bouts of the "practice dreads." This affliction can develop into a daily torture and at times can consume your entire focus. All your energy is directed at how much you don't want to practice or work out. It can affect your studying, your social life, and even your eating habits. I've known athletes whose entire personalities changed prior to a tough day of practice.

At UNC, our off-season football workouts were done in groups according to class schedule. If you were one of those poor souls in the later groups, you would hear from earlier groups about how tough the daily workout had been. Therefore, you endured the pain of a difficult workout twice—first mentally, then physically. (Incidentally, we judged the difficulty of a workout according to the number of guys who threw up!)

The problem here is not the physical part of the workout. Without question, the conditioning program was an essential part of our preparation. The problem is the effect of the mental anguish. The practice dreads can be a major obstacle in getting the most out of your college career. If not properly kept in check, it can prevent you from properly focusing on the task at hand, which will negatively affect your athletic performance, your school work, and your social life.

Positive thinking is the key to avoiding the dreads. If you have set a powerful athletic goal for yourself, then you should view a difficult workout as a means to an end. Be positive, excited, and welcome the challenge of what others have perceived as being a difficult workout. Attack it head-on when the time comes and avoid putting yourself through the workout strain mentally as well as physically.

Remember that your attitude influences your outcomes, so if you want to achieve success, you must be mindful to cultivate a positive outlook.

Turn Obstacles into Opportunities

It was the spring of my freshman year when the new head coach Mack Brown called me into his office. I was

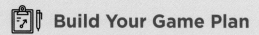 **Build Your Game Plan**

Take a few minutes to write down some examples of when you did or did not keep a positive attitude and how it affected your performance.

1.

2.

3.

4.

5.

nervous. When he became the coach, one of the first things he did was change a bunch of players' positions. But not mine. I was a defensive guy through and through, and unlike most of the guys who played both ways in high school, I had never even taken a snap on offense. I may have been respectful, but I was also a salesman, and if Coach Brown tried to move me to offense, I was ready to convince him otherwise.

When I sat down in his office, I took note that Coach Brown was sitting on the couch next to me. He was a master of communication, including nonverbals. Sitting at your desk is a power play. There are times when it's appropriate. If, however, you want to make someone comfortable, the couch is a better *strategic* choice. It's a "buying sign" that I began to take notice of later, but at the time, all I remember was feeling comfortable. He had a big smile and that raspy Southern accent that always seemed to put people at ease. After a few pleasantries, he said, "After watching you on film, Andy, the thing that stands out is you *explode* off the ball." I couldn't help but smile. I didn't think he even watched film of anyone besides the quarterbacks. He had my attention as he said, "I've also noticed that you are most effective when you move straight ahead. And after talking to the strength coach, I wasn't surprised to learn that you have some of the strongest legs on the team."

So here I was, an eighteen-year-old freshman who was made to feel like a piece of meat by the previous coaching staff, and the new head coach not only had noticed me but also was complimenting me. He instantly won my complete loyalty. If he had told me that he wanted me to jump into a frozen lake, I would have done it! What he actually told me was that the best position for me to utilize my skills was offensive guard. I walked out of that room pumped up. The "speech" that I had prepared about why I should stay on defense was a memory.

When I got to my locker, Dwight Hollier, whose locker was right next to mine, said to me, "What's the big smile for Big Dink?" I told him about my position change, and as the news spread, I learned that I was one of thirty players whose positions had been changed. I also learned that about half of these guys fell into the "bitcher" category and the other half into the "opportunist" category.

In the opportunist category were Torin Dorn, a star running back who had moved to cornerback; Reggie Clark, a star receiver who had been moved to linebacker; Brian Bollinger, a 240-pound tight end who had been moved to offensive tackle; and Deems May, a high school all-American quarterback who had started as a freshman who was being moved to tight end. Do you know what all four of those guys have in common? They all went on to play in the NFL. They were opportunists.

In the bitcher category was a bunch of guys with names you have never heard. These guys only talked about how they got screwed by the "system" and how they would never get a fair shake now that the coaches who recruited them were gone. They flocked to each other like fleas. Silently, they made a pact: they were going to find a way to keep their scholarships without doing any work. The bitchers figured that their football careers were over, so they'd just go through the motions and keep their scholarships. I even heard one guy say that being on scholarship was better than working in McDonald's. Some guys even faked injuries to get out of practice.

What are some of the qualities that define opportunists?
- Opportunists have mentors.
- Opportunists start each day with an accomplishment.
- Opportunists make someone else's day.
- Opportunists reflect on their past success and learn from it.
- Opportunists celebrate their success. It's more fun than mourning defeat.
- Opportunists surround themselves with people who make them feel good about themselves.
- Opportunists think and act in a manner that would make their parents, mentors, coaches, and fans proud.
- Opportunists are grateful, and they say so.
- Opportunists know the importance of love. Self-love breeds self-confidence. Self-confidence breeds success.
- Opportunists don't make excuses.

How can you tell if you are already an opportunist or a bitcher? One way is to start by assessing whether or not the people you surround yourself with are the right people.

Stay Positive

My teammates who failed to complete a difficult workout were usually the same ones every time. The reason they failed was not the result of poor physical conditioning; it was due to poor mental preparation. Even before the workout had begun, these players were talking about how much trouble they were going to have making it. Guess what? They did have trouble.

I have seen too many good athletes burn themselves out from all the mental torturing. I knew athletes who couldn't sleep well or enjoy their time away from the sport because of all the mental anguish they put themselves through. Use positive thinking to conquer these fears. It will allow you to

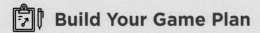

Build Your Game Plan

Describe your five closest peers. What you say about them has a lot to say about you.

1.

2.

3.

4.

5.

accomplish a great deal more in athletics and during your time away from sports.

How do you interpret the so-called "hardships" in your life? Does a bad practice where your coach yells at you make you stronger and wiser, or does it prevent you from doing your best at the next practice? Your reaction will be determined by your attitude. As the saying goes, attitude is everything. Attitude affects your health, your personality, your relationships, your income, your happiness, and your sports performance. While most people recognize the importance of having a good attitude, only the very top achievers have a game plan for maintaining a positive attitude.

Positive thinking and a great attitude make your dreams become reality. Just as negative thoughts can prevent you from reaching your full potential, positive thoughts can bring you to a level higher than you could ever imagine. Show me an overachiever, and I'll show you a positive thinker. Like most things in life, positive thinking is habit forming. Thus, the more success you have, the more likely you are to have a positive attitude. Of course, success comes only with hard work.

The best way for a student-athlete to keep a positive attitude again goes back to goal setting. Let's say your goal is to run faster than you ever have before. Why wouldn't you relish the opportunity of getting up early to work on your skills? I realize this can't always be the case. There are going to be occasions when even the most committed athlete will not be in the mood to work out. However, a positive thinker can usually overcome this by quickly refocusing on their goal.

My main point on the subject of positive thinking is this: most of the practices and workouts you have are going to be mandatory. Since you are required to participate, why not have a good attitude about it? Focus on the benefit. Think about the sense of accomplishment you will have after it is over. Challenge yourself with short-term goals pertaining to the workout. Get the most out of every opportunity.

Remember this: you can never go back and make up a missed or poor workout. The opportunity has been lost. That is why it is so important to do your best at all times. I think a teammate of mine summed it up best when he said to me prior to a grueling workout on a ninety-degree summer day, "Andy, I just go as long and as hard as I can. If I pass out, I know I'll wake up in a cool hospital bed with an IV in my arm and a pretty nurse taking care of me." That phrase got me through a lot of difficult workouts. Maybe it will work for you too. Here are some other ways to help you maintain a positive attitude:

- Surround yourself with positive things—pictures, trophies, quotes, etc.
- Surround yourself with positive people.
- Read and listen to positive books.
- Say all things in a positive way—how you can, not why you can't.
- Believe you can achieve it.
- Don't listen to others who tell you you're nuts. They're just jealous.
- Mentor others.
- Count your blessings, including your health.
- Start now and work at it every day. It's simple, yes, but it does take hard work.

⟳▶ Replay

Your attitude determines how you perceive and then experience your world. If you have a positive attitude and see everything as an opportunity to learn and grow, that is the experience you will have.

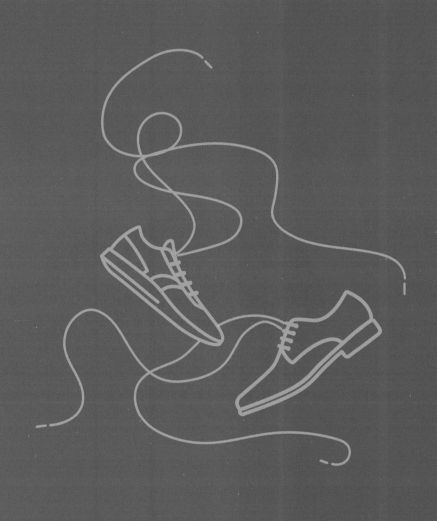

CHAPTER

9

The Only Black Guy in the Room

I believe the advice I've provided throughout this book applies equally to all student-athletes regardless of race, ethnicity, gender, gender identity, sexual preference, religion, or what have you. But I also feel it is particularly important to address racial disparity and the unique challenges brown and black people may face as they enter the workforce. So I asked my friend and former teammate Michael Benefield, a long-time banking executive, to write a chapter from his perspective and experience as an African American.

By Michael Benefield

As this book was being finalized, my college "roomie" approached me and said that he thought he was just about finished, but something was missing. He said this book was written from his perspective, based on his experiences as a white student-athlete, and he didn't feel that it spoke to the experiences of a black student-athlete.

As you know, a great coach can bring a bunch of guys together from different walks of life and coach them to achieve a common goal without regard for race, socioeconomic background, or religion. These coaches know that athletes are more alike than they are different, with the common denominator being a relentless focus on winning and pursuing championships. After your playing days are behind you, however, you will exit the sanctity of that locker room one last time to face the world without your teammates, and this is where life begins for you. And that is what this book is all about—how to leverage the energy, relationships, and currency that you have as a student-athlete on campus to springboard into your future once you leave campus.

This chapter is very timely for me because I just returned from dropping my oldest son off at school to begin his college career as a student-athlete. I'd like to share with you what I shared with him on the ride up. And I wish I were sitting where you are today while someone dropped this knowledge on me.

I have spent the last nineteen years in the private sector at a well-known financial institution and have worked my way up to senior management. As I climbed the corporate ladder, I learned real quickly that fewer and fewer guys looked like me the farther I climbed. Even today as I write, I still walk into meeting rooms where I'm the only black guy in the room. Of course, this comes with a tremendous amount of pressure to always perform well and carry the burden of responsibility for those who follow. My white colleagues don't notice this burden, because everyone in the room looks like them; so no pressure. You see, it's all about how comfortable others feel around you, or how comfortable or uncomfortable they are made to feel by your sheer presence.

I'll tell you like I told my son: once your playing days are over, no one will really care that you were a former student-athlete except those closest to you, such as your family and friends. However, people will care and pay very close attention to three things. Since you look different, you will stick out the minute you enter a room, and people will make evaluations based on their perceptions of you. Therefore, make sure that you are very secure in these three areas and focus your energies on the following:

- Communicate clearly.
- Look the part.
- Build your brand.

So what does this mean, and what's in it for you as a black student-athlete?

Communicate Clearly

When I was in college, an E.F. Hutton financial services commercial was running on TV. The tagline was "when E.F. Hutton talks, everybody listens." Basically, this guy's financial advice was so good, whenever he talked the whole room stopped to listen to what would come next, and you didn't want to miss it. Well, guess what—as a black student-athlete, you are like E.F. Hutton, except people don't want to hear your financial advice; they want to hear if you can string a sentence together and engage in conversation. If you take nothing from this book, take this: you need to have a good, firm handshake and demonstrate strong communication skills both orally and in writing. Bottom line—good diction will take you far. At the end of the day, people need to be able to understand you and what you're saying.

Believe it or not, the initial handshake and how you introduce yourself sets the tone for your conversation. You don't want to speak in rhythms and rhymes, and lose people in a lullaby of *ums, uhs, likes,* and *you knows.* Trust me, it's not a good look and will not go over well in your first job interview if you are challenged in your communication skills. Therefore, I encourage you to practice your introduction. Seize this critical moment to tell them who you are and why you're there. This, more often than not, will set the tone for the discussion and dictate whether or not you get invited back for that second interview.

When you walk into that room and take a seat at the table, people have already made several evaluations and formulated certain perceptions about you. Unfortunately, as a result of how "black folks" are portrayed in the media, most of what people perceive may be negative. Don't fuel their fears or confirm their perceptions with poor diction; this only makes them uncomfortable. See, the key to maintaining relationships is good communication, and communication is the foundation of all good relationships.

Seize the opportunity you have while still on campus to communicate often with alumni after games and with coaches, fans, students, parents of your teammates, professors, counselors, and others. Now is your time! At no other point in life will people be more accepting of you as a black student-athlete than they are now. As a student-athlete, everyone wants to be around you, be your friend, get close to you, and take selfies with you because everyone likes a winner. While you're on this stage for the next two to three years, leverage your celebrity and harness this moment in time to build as many relationships and make as many contacts as possible, so people get to know you for something other than what you might do on Saturday afternoons. The sooner you begin to do this while on campus, the better off you'll be in the long run, which is the ultimate goal. Sadly, once you graduate, the student-athlete title disappears, and guess what you're left with … what people see when you walk into the room.

Look the Part

Now, don't stop reading because you think this next segment is about me telling you how to dress. However, I will tell you that many professions have uniforms. Doctors wear scrubs, painters wear white, and guys in corporate America typically wear suits. Depending upon the profession you choose, there may or may not be a high tolerance for people to express their individuality through how they choose dress for work. Even where I work, your level in the company dictates how you go to work every day. Therefore, a dark suit, white shirt, and cap-toe shoes are the norm for me.

For most black student-athletes, I know it's cool right now to have the earrings and nose rings, body piercings, tattoos, the twists, the locs, and the colored hair. That's all good, and college is a great place to experiment. Heck, I even had a crazy haircut and experimented with different looks while I was in school, so I get it. However, throughout my career, I also learned that when you're the only black guy in the room, people are formulating opinions about you based on your appearance alone, even before you open your mouth to speak.

In the final analysis, whatever you decide to do, make sure you look the part. I once had a guy tell me to dress for the job you want, not the job that you have. Bottom line: if I wanted to be a manager, I had to look like a manager. From that day forward, I took his advice and invested in a few white shirts and a dark suit, and my appearance (in addition to my performance) put me on the right track to advancement within the company. So again, as you start to think about your future, ask yourself if you can wear a suit every day, whether you like to work outdoors or indoors, and whether or not you like wearing sweats and dri-fit gear all day. Again, it's your choice, but whatever you decide, just ensure that you look the part and not like someone who doesn't belong there.

Build Your Brand

All the things that I've shared—having great communication skills, making a statement with your presence and how you look, building good relationships, and doing good work—add up to the sum total of your brand. Your brand is the unique combination of who you are, what you represent, and what others think of you based upon their interactions with you.

At the end of your four to five years of being a student-athlete, who you know and how you know them paves the road for your next move. Again, as I discussed previously, it's about building strong relationships while in school, making people comfortable with being in your presence, and getting to know you as a person outside of your sport. Whether it's grad school, the NFL, or launching a career somewhere, your reputation will and should precede you.

As you start to think about your brand, I'm talking about the reputation that you have established through making connections with others on campus, through working a summer job, through volunteering, or whatever. It all boils down to who you are. Are you the one who shows up early and stays late, or are you always late and looking to leave

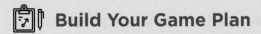

Build Your Game Plan

Identify the professionals whom you already know who can help mentor you and make introductions to other professionals. This includes parents of your high school friends, members of your church, your little league coaches, or former teachers. They all want to help; you simply have to ask. Start by making your list, then contact each individual to schedule a meeting.

Name	Phone Number	Email Address

early? Are you that person who works hard in the weight room in the off-season, or are you the one who looks to cut reps? Do your teammates trust you? Do your coaches trust you? Are you reliable, respectful of others, and respectful of yourself? How you answer these questions makes no difference at all. What makes the greatest impact is how those around you answer these questions; this is what formulates your brand identity. Therefore, I encourage you to work hard to establish your brand, whatever you think that may be at this time. More importantly, if you need to build or repair your brand, think very carefully about how you would like others to perceive you, and be authentic in how you maintain the integrity of your brand. Remember, at the end of the day, whatever your brand, you own it!

So why is your brand so important? Over the years I've learned that when decisions about you are being made, you won't be in the room or even in the building. Are you involved in discussions about where you fall currently on the depth chart? Of course not. The coaches make those decisions. The same will be true once you graduate. When discussions take place about your next career move, ironically, you will not be within five miles of that discussion when the decision is finally made. Many of these important decisions about your career will boil down to one thing: your brand and what it says about your potential to take on more responsibility.

To maintain your brand identity, you will need the help of others. Now is the time to start building those relationships and identifying the people you want in your corner. So when your college career ends, you have people who will not only market and validate your brand but also advocate on your behalf. Remember that you will not always be that black student-athlete, and once you lose the student-athlete title, you need to have something to fall back on that makes people feel comfortable. I encourage you to find that coach, professor, alumnus, or parent who can help guide you in the direction of your dreams. Who knows, perhaps now that you have all this knowledge, I may no longer be the only black guy in the room, so I look forward to seeing you in there!

▶ Replay

How you look, what you say, and how you say it, both online and in person, have a major impact on your personal brand. It's always best to be inclusive, positive, and thoughtful in what you say and what you do.

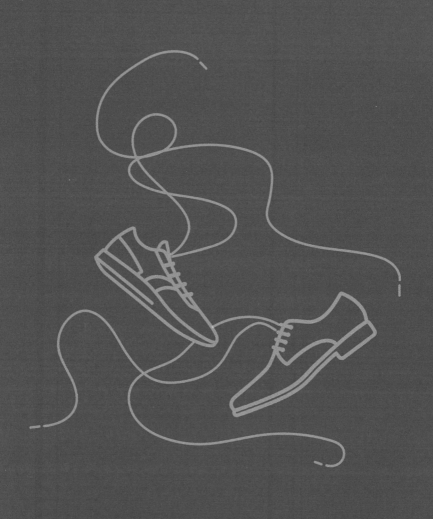

CHAPTER

10

Create Your Future—It's Your Choice

'm almost thirty years removed from playing college sports, but a week doesn't pass that something doesn't come up in a business or social setting about my connection to my university and my accomplishments as an athlete. As I've said throughout this book, people like to be connected to sports, and they like to talk sports with athletes, even former ones like me.

I use my status as a former college student-athlete to build new and stronger relationships, and it has enriched my life and advanced my career. These are some specific things I've done that have been most effective and that you should implement when you graduate:

- Join your school's booster club and be an active attendee and volunteer. Seek a position of leadership. Anyone who shows up at a booster club event will love to meet you and help you. If you are shy, volunteer to work the check-in desk. It guarantees that you will meet everyone in attendance.

- Attend school reunions and homecomings.
- Make a concerted effort to stay in touch with your former teammates and coaches.
- Stay visible on social media specific to your school and school athletics.
- Send your coach an annual holiday card.
- Offer to help current student-athletes with their career pursuits.

My goal in writing this book was to make you, the college student-athlete, aware of the opportunity that has been presented. You are in an excellent position to create a great future for yourself. Set some clear goals for yourself and let nothing stand in the way of reaching them. Strive to be the best athlete, student, and person that you can be. Remember to work hard at the little things on a daily basis, even when nobody else is watching. This is the sign of a true winner and will make you a success in all walks of life.

Also keep in mind that being different is good. Be the most positive person you know. Be polite and courteous. Write thank-you notes whenever appropriate. Do favors for your friends and ask for nothing in return. Become a well-thought-of role model for kids in your community. (College athletes have gotten a bad "rap" as of lately. Please do your part in dispelling the notion that athletes are spoiled and over-glamorized.) Be a prized member of society by being kind and honest with people.

Above all else, don't let college athletics use you; instead, use college athletics. Use it to get a great education. Use it to make friends who can only be made through the commonality of sportsmanship. Use it to open doors that will help you get a good job. And most importantly, use it to have a tremendous amount of fun.

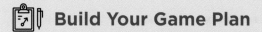

Build Your Game Plan

List on- and off-campus clubs and events you can participate in after graduation to continue taking advantage of your college network.

1.
2.
3.
4.
5.
6.
7.
8.
9.
10.

Life is too short not to enjoy as much of it as possible. Sure, you're going to have tough times, but grow from them. Find something positive in your defeats. Learn from your mistakes and do better the next time. Keeping things in perspective is the key element.

Your success or failure is the responsibility of just one person—*you*. Not your coaches, not your teachers, not your significant other, not your parents, not your friends, not your enemies, not your competitors—*just you*.

Maybe you're thinking, "I just need a lucky break." Well, make your own break. Work harder, study more, put yourself around winners, and improve your attitude. Do whatever it takes. You already know what it will take to make your vision a reality. Just execute it.

I hope you get as much out of the college athletic experience as I did. Nothing is more special to me than my college years. Keep in mind that the time goes quickly. Stay focused on your goals and don't waste a minute. Keep the Main Thing the Main Thing, and don't get distracted by meaningless pursuits.

You now have a game plan you can come back to again and again, not just for landing your first job but also to advance in your career. Having good mentors, a proactive networking strategy, and an attractive personal brand are things that become even more important as you strive for career advancement. Use what you've learned to fast-track to the top.

And even though your playing days will soon be over, the "ex" student-athlete label remains forever. You'll be eighty years old, and people will still reference that you played a sport in college. Plus, you're part of a network of both the general alumni and former athletes from your school, and your status as a former athlete gives you the advantage of being able to make friends quickly with successful people.

You've worked harder than most to get to this point in your life. I urge you to put in just a little more work to implement the Game Plan you've created. Rev your engine hard now so you can soar for the next fifty years. The choice is yours.

▶ Replay

Going pro in life really is about leveraging your student-athlete experience for success after college. New life. New lifestyle. New uniform. New rules. New ball game. *Same success principles.* You have all the tools for a great future. Go for it!

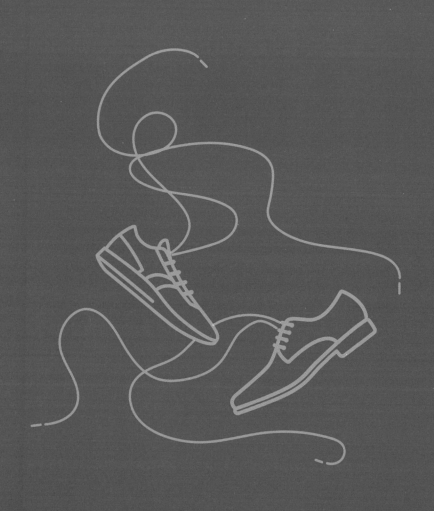

Recommended Reading

- *How to Win Friends and Influence People,*
  Dale Carnegie

- *The 7 Habits of Highly Effective People,*
  Stephen Covey

- *The Four Agreements: A Practical Guide to Personal
  Freedom,* Don Miguel Ruiz

- *Getting Things Done,* David Allen

- *Think and Grow Rich,* Napoleon Hill

About the Author

Andy Dinkin is a commercial real estate broker and entrepreneur. He was a football scholarship athlete at the University of North Carolina at Chapel Hill playing under Coach Mack Brown. His athletic experience shaped the principles by which he lives: honesty, teamwork, and having a positive attitude. Andy is a member of the Rotary Club of Charlotte, the Metrolina Business Council, and the Charlotte Region Commercial Board of Realtors. He serves on the board of the Charlotte Torah Center and previously served on the board of Girls on the Run International. In his free time, he enjoys attending Bruce Springsteen concerts, taking road trips to Chapel Hill, losing his fantasy football league, playing with his kids, and completing his wife's honey-do list.

Invite Andy to Speak

 andy@goingproinlife.com

Connect with Andy

andydinkin

goingproinlife.com